Supporting Children with Medical Conditions

Hull Learning Services

 David Fulton Publishers

David Fulton Publishers Ltd
The Chiswick Centre, 414 Chiswick High Road, London W4 5TF

www.fultonpublishers.co.uk

First published in Great Britain by Hull Learning Services

David Fulton Publishers is a division of Granada Learning Limited, part of ITV plc.

British Library Cataloguing in Publication Data
A catalogue record for this book is available from the British Library.

ISBN 1 84312 224 3

Typeset by Matrix Creative, Wokingham
Printed and bound in Great Britain

Contents

Section 3: Access to the curriculum

Section 4: Developing skills for learning

Foreword

This book has been produced in partnership with Hull City Council's Education Service for Physical Disability and Special Educational Needs Support Service and the Hull and District Cerebral Palsy Society. Guidance has also been received from a number of health professionals within the Hull and East Riding Health Authority. It was written by:

Susan Coulter, ESPD
Lesley Kynman, ESPD
Elizabeth Morling, SENSS
Francesca Murray, Hull and District Cerebral Palsy Society

It is one of a series of eleven titles providing an up-to-date overview of special educational needs for Special Educational Needs Co-ordinators (SENCOs), teachers, classroom assistants and other professionals and parents.

It is hoped that the information in this book will give an overview of a variety of medical conditions, give educational implications and provide some suggestions to enable teachers and other school staff to support pupils.

For details of other titles and how to order, please see page 133.

Acknowledgements

We extend our grateful thanks to:

Dr Ashraf, Staff Grade Paediatrician

Joy Donaldson, Paediatric Physiotherapist

Margaret Riley, Paediatric Palliative Care Co-ordinator

Hilary Linford, Paediatric Specialist Diabetic Nurse

Hull and East Riding Community Disability Nurse Team for their invaluable advice and support

Senior Adviser John Hill for his support and encouragement throughout the development of this series.

Introduction

The majority of pupils with medical conditions are educated in their local mainstream schools. Their conditions are usually such that they can access the full curriculum when consideration is given to their individual medical needs. A small number of pupils who have medical conditions may be educated in a special school environment but the medical condition is not usually their primary special educational need.

"A medical diagnosis... does not necessarily imply SEN... It is the child's educational needs rather than diagnosis that must be considered."7:64 SENDA 2001

Children with a medical condition come within the remit of the Special Educational Needs and Disability Act 2001 (SENDA 2001) when their condition 'has a substantial and long-term adverse effect on his or her ability to carry out normal day-to-day activities'. Not all children fall within this description; however, schools have a duty to anticipate the needs of children with a medical condition.

"A person has a disability... if he has a physical or mental impairment that has a substantial and long-term adverse effect on his ability to carry out normal day-to-day activities." Section 1(1), Disability Discrimination Act 1995

Implications of the Disability Discrimination Act (1995) as amended by the Special Educational Needs and Disability Act 2001 (SENDA 2001)

The Act:

- strengthens the right of children to be educated in mainstream schools;

- requires LEAs to arrange for parents and/or children with SEN to be provided with advice on SEN matters, and also a means of settling disputes with schools and LEAs (parent partnership services and mediation schemes);

- requires schools to tell parents where they are making special educational provision for their child and allows schools to request a statutory assessment of a pupil's needs.

To support inclusion SENDA 2001 recommends that:

- Schools should make reasonable adjustments to accommodate pupils with SEN so they are not disadvantaged by their condition.

- This may involve revising policies and practices so that they take the educational implications of medical conditions into consideration.

- Schools must also evaluate their curriculum delivery, especially the way written information is presented, to make it accessible to all pupils.

Section 1

Medical conditions and possible educational implications

Definition, cause and treatment of anaphylactic shock (anaphylaxis)

Definition

Anaphylaxis is an acute allergic reaction requiring immediate medical attention.

Cause

It is most commonly triggered by substances to which the pupil is sensitive, e.g. nuts; eggs; milk; shellfish; certain drugs; venom from stinging insects.

Symptoms

Symptoms will vary from individual to individual and will depend on what type of contact there has been with the substance causing the allergic reaction.

Symptoms can include:

- itching;
- strange metallic taste in the mouth; sensation of burning or itching of the tongue, lips, throat;
- swelling of the face, lips, tongue with or without difficulty in swallowing;
- skin blotches;
- generalised flushing of the skin;
- abdominal cramps or nausea;
- increased heart rate;
- difficulty in breathing;
- sudden feeling of weakness (dizziness/fainting);
- collapse;
- unconsciousness.

Few pupils would experience all these symptoms.

Treatment

- Avoid substances which are known to cause a reaction;
- use of Epipen (adrenaline) to reverse the reaction.

For further information contact:

The Anaphylaxis Campaign
PO Box 275
Farnborough GU14 7SX

Tel: 01252 542029   www.anaphylaxis.org.uk

Educational implications

(anaphylactic shock)

Staff training and administrative issues

DfEE circular 14/96 "Supporting Children with Medical Needs" provides the legal framework that schools are required to work within. It contains advice and pro-formas for school use.

- Medical training should be arranged for staff who have volunteered to administer medication in an emergency. This is usually in the form of Epipen.
- A clear procedure should be established for summoning an ambulance in an emergency.
- A foolproof mechanism should be established for the sharing of information with all staff that comes into contact with the pupil.

Food management issues

- School meals – the catering supervisor needs to be aware of the pupil's requirements in relation to the menu. A packed lunch provided by the family may be preferable to a school meal.
- Snacks and treats in the classroom and playground – staff and pupils should be made aware that some pupils may not be able to share such treats.
- Science and food technology experiments with food – these curriculum areas may cause difficulty for the pupil who is at risk of anaphylaxis. Suitable alternative arrangements should be made.

Individual health care plan

The individual health care plan should be drawn up with the parents and school nurse if possible. The following points should be considered:

- definition of the allergy;
- emergency procedure to be followed;
- treatment;
- food management;
- precautionary measures;
- staff training;
- staff indemnity;
- parental consent and agreement.

See photocopiable Individual Health Care Plan (IHCP) page 127.

Arthrogryposis

Definition

Arthrogryposis or Arthrogryposis Multiplex Congenita describes a baby born with multiple joint contractures (a contracture is a limitation in the range of movement of a joint). It covers a wide range of conditions, Amyoplasia being the most common form. This is not a hereditary condition but Distal Arthrogryposis has a genetic basis. The incidence of Arthrogryposis is 1 in 10,000 births.

Children with arthrogryposis may be characterised by the internal rotation of the hands, sloping shoulders and long, tapering fingers; however the positions of feet, knees and hips are variable. In some children only two or three joints are affected, but in others all joints, including the spine and jaw are affected. Most children will be within the normal range of cognitive ability.

Causes

A number of factors can affect the normal development of the joint and cause the fixation:

- muscle defects caused by the failure of muscles to form or function normally in the womb or by a degenerative process taking place at this time;
- abnormal connective tissue or joints causing limited movement;
- a neurological deficit caused by absent, abnormal or malfunctioning nerves;
- insufficient space in the womb for the foetus to move as a result of an abnormal womb shape, insufficient fluid or more than one developing foetus.

Treatment

- early diagnosis is very important to enable treatment to start as soon as possible;
- physiotherapy should start immediately to develop a programme of passive stretching combined with the use of splints;
- serial plasters and corrective surgery can complement physiotherapy as the child grows;
- lightweight orthoses may help standing and walking;
- improvement of hand function is sometimes achieved through surgical intervention;
- many children improvise and learn ways to overcome their own difficulties.

For further information contact:
TAG (The Arthrogryposis Group)
1, The Oaks, Gillingham,
Kent SP8 4SW
www.tagonline.org.uk

Educational implications (arthrogryposis)

As with all medical conditions the severity of this condition can vary. Some pupils remain ambulant throughout their school days whilst others may require a wheelchair to aid mobility. It may be necessary to consider the following points when planning to include a pupil with arthrogryposis:

- plan classroom allocation taking restricted mobility into account;
- be aware that the pupil may have difficulty in climbing stairs;
- the pupil is likely to have difficulty sitting on the floor during carpet time and assemblies;
- PE lessons may require differentiation, consult with the occupational therapist and physiotherapist for advice;
- a physical management routine may need to be incorporated in the school day: consider by whom, where and when this will be implemented;
- manipulation of standard classroom equipment can be difficult if arms and hands are affected;
- limited recording abilities may necessitate use of specialised fine motor equipment and the early introduction to word processing skills;
- reorganise positioning of equipment in the classroom to aid independent access;
- support the pupil in organisation of their personal effects, such as school bag;
- facilitate disabled toilet access if required;
- carefully consider arrangements for out-of-school visits and work experience placements;
- investigate home school transport if necessary.

Asthma

Definition

Asthma is a condition that affects the airways. The airways are the small tubes that carry air in and out of the lungs. Asthmatic airways are more sensitive than non-asthmatic airways and can react badly when exposed to a cold, viral infection or another trigger.

When this happens the muscles around the walls of the airways tighten, causing the airways to narrow. The lining of the airways becomes inflamed and starts to swell. Sticky mucus or phlegm is produced. This may cause coughing or wheezing. If not treated correctly, asthma can be a very serious condition. Therefore, it is important that medication is taken as directed.

Cause or triggers

A trigger is anything that irritates the airways and causes symptoms of asthma to appear. Everybody is different and may react to one or more triggers. Some of the more common triggers are listed here:

- colds, flu and other viral infections;
- house dust mite;
- cigarette smoking/passive smoking;
- fur and feathers;
- pollen;
- exercise.

Other triggers for asthma can be:

- mould/spores;
- changes in weather;
- changes in emotion – laughter, crying;
- effects of chemicals, such as paints, car fumes, spray deodorants;
- hormones, especially during puberty;
- stress.

Treatment

The treatment of asthma can be divided into the following 3 main groups:

- relievers;
- controllers;
- protectors.

Note: *Only 'blue' reliever inhalers are required in school*

Relievers

These are usually blue in colour and come in a range of devices.

- They are used to relieve symptoms when they occur (they usually take effect within 5–10 minutes).

- Two puffs of a reliever can be used 5–10 minutes before exercise to prevent symptoms occurring.

- Relievers must be carried by the person at all times or be readily available for KS1 pupils.

- The medicine in reliever inhalers will not cause problems if taken by another person. Neither the propellant nor the drug is addictive.

Controllers

These come in a range of devices and are usually coloured brown, orange or red depending on the medicine they contain.

- Controllers reduce swelling in the airways and stop them from being so sensitive.

- Regular use of a controller will reduce the risk of a severe attack.

- Controller medicine needs to be taken regularly, usually twice a day and must be continued until advised otherwise by the doctor.

- The steroids used in controller inhalers are not the same as those used by body builders. The dose is very small and works directly in the lungs where it is needed.

Protectors

Protectors are relatively new in the treatment of asthma. They act in a similar way to relievers, but the drug has a longer lasting effect. They come in two forms:

- inhaler (usually green), which is taken twice a day: this inhaler should never be used as a reliever inhaler;

- tablet form, which is taken either once or twice daily depending on the drug, in addition to inhaler therapy.

For further information contact:
National Asthma Campaign
Providence House
Providence Place
London N1 0NT

www.asthma.org.uk

For detailed advice refer to the book in this series
Supporting Children with Asthma.

Managing an asthma attack

Your aim is: **to ease breathing and seek medical aid if necessary.**

1. Keep calm and reassure the pupil.
2. Let the pupil adopt the position they find most comfortable; this is usually sitting down.
3. Follow the guidelines below for administering treatment:

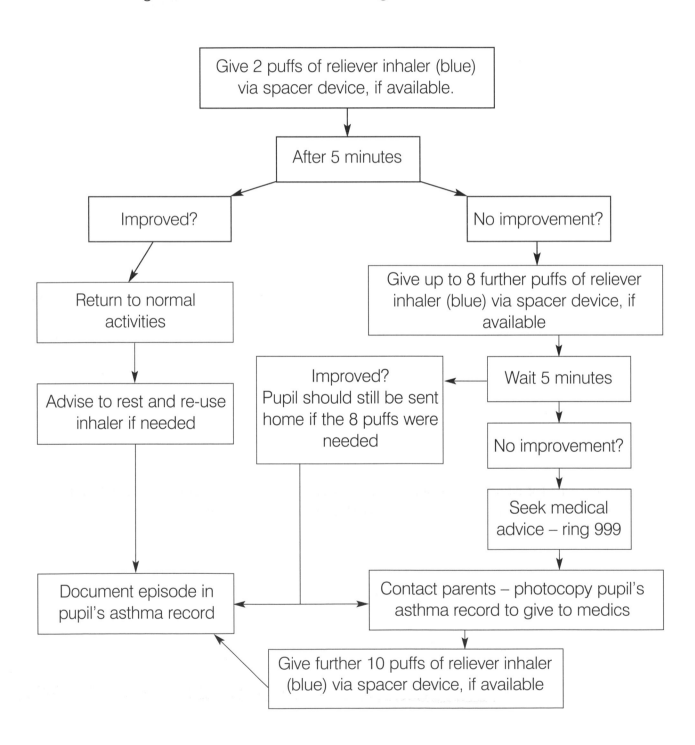

Brittle bone disease

Definition

Brittle bone disease is the common name for a large group of conditions. The most common cause is osteogenesis imperfecta, a range of conditions caused by inherited abnormalities in collagen, the protein structure of bones. The condition can vary in its severity, from a child having multiple fractures to others whose condition may be difficult to identify.

There are four types of osteogenesis imperfecta:

- **Type I** is a milder condition which is characterised by good stature, relatively few fractures and very blue/grey sclera (whites of the eyes).
- **Type II** causes very severe fractures resulting in stillborn babies or death within the first few weeks of life.
- **Type III** is severe, although not life-threatening. However, the child may have markedly impaired growth.
- **Type IV** is as Type I without sclera.

Associated problems may be:

– sweating excessively;	– bruising easily;
– fragile teeth;	– lax joints.

Other less common causes of brittle bone disease include osteopetrosis, hypophosphatasia, fibrous dysplasia (Albright syndrome) and ideopathic juvenile osteoporosis. Temporary brittle bone disease may cause fractures in the first year of life and improve later.

Treatment

There is no cure for brittle bone diseases; however progress is being made with the development of drug treatments. Orthopaedic management and surgery may help.

- Fractures are treated as they occur.
- Plaster casts may be used.
- Physiotherapy will be necessary to reduce the impact of long-term damage.

For further information contact:
Brittle Bone Society
30 Guthrie Street, Dundee DD1 5BS
Tel: 08000 282459   e-mail: bb@brittlebone.org   www.brittlebone.org

Educational implications (brittle bones)

Mobility in and around the school site

Pupils are vulnerable to knocks and bumps that could result in fractures. The pupils and the school need to develop strategies to minimise the risk. Consider:

- supervision of movement at busy times, e.g. change of lesson;
- timing of movement between lessons (leave before or after the other pupils);
- timing of homework instructions if the pupil leaves early;
- finding a quiet, 'safe', social area for use at breaks;
- who will move the pupil's belongings between lessons?

Written work

- The effects of multiple fractures and lax joints can make writing difficult.
- Occupational therapy (OT) input can advise on seating and positioning.
- The pupil's hands may tire quickly and therefore, writing may be slow.
- Use of ICT equipment where it may be helpful in some cases.
- Provide an additional set of books for use at home, to cut down on the weight carried by the pupil.

Art/D&T/Science

- Pupils are rarely static in these lessons. Support may be required to monitor the physical environment and minimise movement around the classroom.
- Care should be taken with regard to weight when handling equipment.

PE

- Most mainstream activities will be unsuitable for pupils with severe asthma.
- Parents and medical staff will advise accordingly.
- Swimming is often recommended.

Other considerations

- Toilet arrangements – pupils may need to use a specialist facility to avoid potential hazards within a communal toilet. Pupils with restricted growth, particularly short arms, may require assistance with cleansing.
- Consider the position within the classroom in relation to ease of access.
- Examinations – special arrangements may be required.
- Protection and over protection – be aware of the tendency to over protect these pupils. Ensure the pupils are given opportunities for social interaction.

- Communication – consider how pupils could contact support staff for assistance, when required out of 'timetabled' time (phone/bleep/walkie talkie).

- Autonomy – encourage the pupils to make decisions themselves.

Raising awareness of the pupil's condition

- Accurate information should be shared with all staff.

- Emergency routines, via individual health care plans (IHCP) should be agreed.

- The pupil's permission should be obtained, to explain the condition to other pupils.

Cerebral palsy

Definition

Cerebral palsy is essentially damage to the brain. One medical definition is that "cerebral palsy is caused by a brain lesion which is non-progressive and leads to variable impairment of the co-ordination of muscle action, with resulting inability of the person to maintain normal movements. However, it may be the case that as a child gets older their needs change" (Scope publications 1996). The term cerebral palsy is a diagnosis that covers a wide range of ability and need. Some pupils with cerebral palsy may be of average or above average ability. They may have physical impairments affecting mobility and co-ordination; speech, chewing and swallowing; sensory impairments such as vision and hearing difficulties. There may be accompanying epilepsy. Other pupils may have moderate to severe learning difficulties accompanied by a range of physical impairments.

- **Spastic cerebral palsy** means that muscles are stiff and difficult to control. Within this definition there can be three types of spastic cerebral palsy. *Hemiplegia* is when either the right or the left side of the body is affected by spasticity; other parts of the body remain unaffected. *Diplegia* is when the legs are affected; the arms are usually unaffected or only slightly so. *Quadriplegia* is when all four limbs are affected.

- **Athetoid cerebral palsy** is when children have difficulty in maintaining a position and make involuntary movements. Since the movements are hard to control, it may take a great deal of effort to achieve a desired action or activity. Speech can be affected, owing to abnormal movements of the oral musculature and vocal cords.

- **Ataxic cerebral palsy** is the least common form of cerebral palsy. The child has unsteadiness of movement and poor balance, walking may be jerky, hands can be shaky, speech development may be slow and spatial awareness may be impaired.

Causes

Cerebral palsy can be caused by an injury to the brain, before, during or after birth. In many cases no one knows for certain what has caused the brain injury.

Treatment

Cerebral palsy cannot be cured. It is non-progressive in that the level of brain damage does not get worse. Pupils with cerebral palsy will have a physical management programme devised by a physiotherapist/occupational therapist, to maximise a pupil's functional abilities. Some pupils may have orthopaedic surgery to release tendons thus improving the range of movement. Others may have botulinum therapy to relax and lengthen specific muscles.

For further information contact:

Scope
PO Box 833
Milton Keynes MK12 5NY
www.scope.org.uk

For details refer to the book in this series *Supporting Children with Cerebral Palsy*.

Educational implications (cerebral palsy)

Not all pupils with cerebral palsy will have learning difficulties. Depending on the part of the brain that has sustained an injury, pupils may experience varying degrees of difficulty in some or all of the following areas:

- mobility;
- co-ordination;
- fine motor skills;
- concentration;
- attention and listening skills;
- visual perception;
- speech and language;
- vision;
- hearing;
- eating and drinking skills;
- dressing;
- toileting.

It is important that an inter-disciplinary approach is adopted when assessing and planning to meet the needs of pupils with cerebral palsy. Strategies are included in later sections of this book. The following points should be taken into consideration:

- restricted mobility necessitating use of a wheelchair or mobility aids;
- difficulty climbing stairs or accessing the first floor in a wheelchair;
- difficulty sitting on the floor during carpet time and assembly;
- PE lessons may require differentiation;
- a physical management routine may need to be incorporated in the school day – when and where will it be implemented?
- time for liaison with outside agencies and funding to release staff for training in the use of specialised equipment;
- manipulation of standard classroom equipment. Is specialised equipment or a compensatory approach required?
- positioning of equipment to aid independent access;
- organisation of personal effects such as the school bag;
- disabled toilet access with support arrangements to assist with personal care issues;
- arrangements for out of school visits with home/school transport if required.

Club foot (talipes)

Definition

There are four known kinds of club foot. The most common is called 'talipes equinus-varus', which describes the heel as being drawn up and turned inwards. Sometimes the condition just affects one foot and at other times, both.

Cause

The condition is more prevalent in boys than girls and although the medical profession has been aware of it for many years, its actual cause is unknown. There is evidence that this condition runs in families and is hereditary.

The position in the womb may determine the type of condition present and there is some suggestion that there are links with a reduced amount of amniotic fluid or 'olighhydramnios'.

Treatment

The condition can be detected prior to birth by ultrasound. However, it is not usually discovered until after the child is born. Although this condition causes stress and anxiety to parents, it is usually treatable with a great deal of success and the child can make equally good physical progress as those children without the condition.

The treatments used in this condition vary with the severity. Treatment will begin soon after the child is diagnosed. Initially, physiotherapy and the strapping of the feet tend to be the more common forms of treatment. It is possible also to use casting rather than strapping. Relapse is possible as children grow and in some more severe cases, surgery will be used. Surgery will involve the lengthening of affected tendons and ligaments and then the limb is put in plaster.

The surgical treatment for talipes is sometimes the same as, or similar to, limb-lengthening surgery. Here, the bones are broken and re-set with a growth space, using an external fixator (metal cage).

> *For further information contact:*
> www.clubfoot.co.uk
>
> http://steps-charity.org.uk/talipes.php

Educational implications (club foot)

Advice is usually available from the orthopaedic department or the physiotherapy department involved in the treatment of pupils with this condition. Pupils, who have had limb-lengthening surgery or talipes surgery, may return to school with an external fixator (metal cage). The family will have received instruction on how to care for the pin sites and how to turn the screws to facilitate gradual lengthening. Schools should not be required to adjust the screws on an external fixator or to care for pin sites. Pupils generally need to have their leg elevated on an extended support attached to a wheelchair.

The following points may need to be taken into consideration when planning for a pupil to return to school following limb-lengthening surgery:

- physical access to the school building and positioning of the classroom on the ground floor;
- access to a toilet sufficiently spacious to accommodate a wheelchair with a leg extension;
- position within the classroom for ease of entry and exit;
- height of tables, to accommodate the extended leg;
- supervision during non-teaching time, e.g. breaks and lunchtimes;
- alternative activities for PE lessons;
- planned absences to attend hospital on a regular basis, which may require 'catch up time';
- where and when physical management routines, recommended by the physiotherapist to prevent muscle wastage during the treatment period, can be implemented;
- if the school's existing resources cannot meet the pupil's needs, advice can be obtained from the LEA;
- if home/school transport is required: LEA to be contacted, if necessary.

Cystic fibrosis

Definition

Cystic Fibrosis (CF) is the most common, life threatening, inherited disease affecting 1:2,500 of the white Caucasian population of the UK. It is a rare condition in other ethnic groups.

Causes

Cystic fibrosis is caused by an abnormal gene on chromosome number seven. Diagnosis usually takes place in early childhood because chest infections and chronic gastro-intestinal malabsorption cause a 'failure to thrive'. A 'sweat test' can detect an abnormal amount of chloride ions. Diagnosis is then confirmed by genetic tests, which can detect one of the recognised CF genes.

Symptoms

Cystic fibrosis is a multi-system disease affecting many organs, mainly the lungs and gut. Mucus is excessively sticky and cannot perform its normal function of removing debris and bacteria from the air passages in the lungs. The symptoms can be:

- a persistent cough;
- excessive saliva and mucus;
- shortness of breath;
- recurrent chest infections;
- recurrent fatty diarrhoea if correct treatment is not received;
- constipation;
- blockage of the bowel resulting in severe pain;
- poor absorption of nutrients leading to poor growth.

Further symptoms may include sinusitis, enlarged liver and spleen, diabetes and fertility problems.

Treatment

- There is no known cure for cystic fibrosis although research is progressing into gene therapy.
- Life expectancy is reduced but the prognosis is improving as treatment develops.
- Regular physiotherapy is needed to clear harmful mucus from the lungs.
- Frequent courses of antibiotics are used to treat recurrent chest infections, taken orally, inhaled through nebulisers or intravenously.

- Pancreas defects are treated by enzyme supplements (in capsule form), which assist the digestion of protein and fat. These are taken in large numbers with meals.

- Other symptoms are treated as necessary.

- Heart/lung transplants have been used with success.

For further information contact:

Cystic Fibrosis Trust
11, London Road
Bromley, Kent BR1 1BY

enquiries@cftrust.org.uk

www.cftr.org

Educational implications (cystic fibrosis)

There is no evidence to suggest that pupils with cystic fibrosis have learning difficulties. However they can be late in reaching developmental milestones due to their early failure to thrive. Academic progress can sometimes be affected by frequent and sometimes prolonged absences from school as a result of chest infections or hospitalisation.

As with other medical conditions, schools should work with other agencies, including medical professionals, to ensure the needs of the pupil are met in the mainstream setting. Most of the physical management routines such as chest physiotherapy are carried out at home. Extra physiotherapy may be required in school when the pupil has a chest infection (training will be given by the physiotherapist).

There are a number of issues which should be considered, when planning to meet the needs of a pupil with cystic fibrosis.

- Access to a small private room when extra physiotherapy or nebuliser treatment is required, should be available.

- Supervision should be provided at lunchtime, for younger children who are not yet able to manage their own medication.

- Be aware that pupils with CF may be teased about their persistent cough, small stature and having to take tablets with all food.

- Full participation in PE lessons is generally recommended because it helps to loosen sputum in the lungs. Be aware that the pupil with CF may feel unusually tired and lethargic following a chest infection.

- Arrangements to minimise infection, such as being allowed to stay inside at breaks during cold damp weather, should be considered.

- Older pupils may have portable intravenous antibiotic equipment. PE and boisterous play may not be recommended, if this equipment is in use.

- Examination concessions may need to include:
    - additional time up to 25%;
    - administration of treatment during a supervised break;
    - arrangements to take examinations outside school e.g. hospital/home.

- A record of health related absences should be kept as evidence for the examination boards.

- Careers advisers may wish to contact the Cystic Fibrosis Trust Support Service for advice relating to career and job prospects. Pupils with CF can cope with most jobs except those that are physically demanding or environmentally unsuitable.

- Normal rebellious adolescent behaviour can have serious consequences for the teenager with CF. Faddy diets and neglected physiotherapy are common issues.

- Older pupils may be in denial of the potential seriousness of the condition. This is a coping mechanism; sympathetic understanding and counselling may be needed. Caution is advised when offering counselling. Pastoral staff should check with parents about how much knowledge the pupil has about his or her condition and how much the parents want them to have.

- Delayed onset of puberty may cause anxiety: boys are likely to be infertile although not impotent, and girls can have serious health problems if they become pregnant.

- The psychological pressures arising from the chronic nature of the condition will affect the whole family.

Diabetes

Definition

Diabetes Mellitus is a common condition which occurs when the amount of sugar in the blood is too high and cannot be used properly by the body.

Blood sugar comes from sweet sugary foods and starchy foods such as potatoes and bread. Some meats such as liver also produce these sugars. Insulin, made by the pancreas, helps to provide energy for the body. Insulin would normally control the amount of sugar in the blood; levels of insulin fall during activity.

There are two types of Diabetes. Type 1 develops when the body is unable to produce insulin; it is known as insulin dependent diabetes and usually occurs before the age of forty. Type 2 is when the body produces insufficient insulin; it is known as non insulin dependent diabetes and usually occurs after the age of forty.

Causes

The condition occurs when the pancreatic cells that produce the insulin, are destroyed. Although the actual cause is not known, it is thought to be triggered by some viruses or infections.

Symptoms of diabetes are generally:

- extreme thirst
- excessive passing of urine
- extreme fatigue

- blurred or affected vision
- thrush

The condition does develop fairly quickly, more in weeks than months, and symptoms are very evident.

Treatment

Treatment for diabetes tries to maintain blood sugar levels and blood pressure level as near to normal as possible. It also aims to protect against long-term damage to the eyes; kidneys; nerves; heart and major arteries. Diabetes is usually treated by insulin injections and attention to diet. Sometimes those with the condition need other medication/tablets.

For further information contact:
Diabetes UK Central Office
10 Queen Anne Street
London W1 G9LH
Tel: 020 7323 1531   www.diabetes.org.uk   email: info@diabetes.org.uk

---

Educational implications (diabetes)

The pupil with diabetes will require an individual health care plan.

- Pupils may need to monitor their blood sugar levels at school. It should be decided in conjunction with the pupil, where this is carried out, i.e. in the classroom or away from it. A blood sugar check involves pricking the finger and putting a drop of blood onto a test strip.

- Schools should consider where the blood sugar checking kit, insulin and snacks will be stored.

- Younger pupils will require support to administer tests but older pupils should be able to administer tests themselves.

- Pupils may need to inject insulin during the school day. An appropriate place should be assigned (the toilet area is not suitable). Safe disposal of materials should be available.

- Pupils with diabetes should have access to drinks of water when they require them.

- Pupils may need to visit the toilet more frequently. It should be accepted that the pupil be allowed to go when necessary, without seeking permission. A discreet system should be in place, e.g. placing a token on the teacher's desk to ensure they are aware of the pupil's absence from the room.

- Pupils will require a snack at break time or in lesson time as a part of their medical care. (It is the family's responsibility to provide this).

- Pupils should participate in PE lessons. However, this can lower blood sugar levels. They may need to take an extra snack before or after participating.

- Pupils should be able to participate in out-of-school trips. A planning meeting will be necessary with parents, particularly if an overnight stay is involved. Ensure all equipment, medication and snacks used at home are readily available throughout the residential visit. The individual health care plan which addresses the pupil's needs must be carried. Further information can be obtained by contacting the pupil's named diabetes specialist nurse.

- Pupils may need a meal plan. Parents should ensure that the school is notified of dietary needs. A paediatric dietician will contact schools, if there are any special dietary requirements. When possible, pupils with diabetes should be allowed first sitting at lunch.

First aid/emergency responses

School staff should be aware of signs and symptoms, which indicate that a pupil may need to receive emergency treatment:

Hypoglycaemia (low blood sugar) is caused by:

insufficient food;
unusual amount of exercise;
excess insulin;
delayed meal;
stress;
hot weather.

Signs and symptoms	Treatment
– mood change; – loss of concentration; – shaking; – headache; – dizziness; – sweating; – pale appearance; – glazed eyes; – hunger.	Fast-acting sugar should be given immediately to raise the blood glucose level, e.g. – sugary drinks – lemonade (not diet); – fresh fruit juice; – glucose tablets; – small chocolate bar; – 'hypo stop' – given by parents. *It is the family's responsibility to make these available and replenish supplies.*

If a pupil is confused he/she may need help, i.e. sugary items mentioned above or 'hypo stop' should be rubbed inside the cheek. **N.B.** This should not be done if the pupil is unconscious.

After recovery (about 10 or 15 minutes) the pupil will need starchy food, e.g. milk and biscuits or a sandwich. He/she may have a headache, feel sick or tired.

Hyperglycaemia (high blood pressure) can occur as part of diabetes. A detailed IHCP should be written in consultation with the diabetes nurse and the parents, to address this and other medical issues.

Severe hyperglycaemia is a medical emergency

Signs and symptoms	Treatment
– unresponsive; – unconscious; – failure to respond to glucose.	– Ensure the pupil will not harm him/herself; – put into recovery position; – call an ambulance; – treat as in the IHCP.

Eczema

Definition

Eczema describes a group of skin conditions, affecting all ages. Those affecting children include atopic eczema, allergic contact dermatitis, irritant contact dermatitis and infantile seborrhoeic dermatitis.

It is thought that 20% of school aged children have eczema and one in twelve adults continue to be affected.

The severity of eczema can vary from mild cases where the skin is hot and itchy, to severe cases where the skin is broken, raw and bleeding.

Cause

The causes can be very varied. Atopic eczema is thought to be hereditary. It is also believed that people with atopic eczema are sensitive to allergens in the environment. In these cases the child often has asthma and hay fever. Other types of eczema can be caused by irritants such as chemicals and detergents.

Treatment

- Minimising environmental allergens can help.
- External medications such as cortisone cream, ointments, lotions or tars can be used to treat the condition.
- Itching can be relieved by antihistamines.
- Secondary infections may require antibiotic treatment.
- Cortisone can be given in pill or injection form, when other medications fail.
- A new class of drugs known as topical immunomodulators (TIMS) has recently become available to treat moderate eczema.

For further information contact:
National Eczema Society
Hill House
Highgate Hill
London N19 5NA
Tel: 0870 241 3604 (Eczema Information Service)

www.eczema.org

Educational implications (eczema)

Skin conditions, such as eczema, can cause severe discomfort and distress for some pupils. Eczema is sometimes exacerbated by stress. This leads to frantic itching, resulting in damage and bleeding to the affected areas.

The following advice relates to general issues for consideration when planning the management of this condition in schools. Any proposed changes to the current care regime must be fully discussed with the parents and included within an individual health care plan. Help in drawing up a health care plan may be sought from the school nurse and the parents.

- Pupils should be encouraged to participate in all activities.

- They should be encouraged to develop the ability to identify occasions/activities when their skin will need extra attention.

- Careful monitoring of skin reactions to specific activities is necessary. Close liaison with parents is advised.

- Some pupils benefit from the use of emollient creams as a barrier or preventive measure, to be used before playing with sand, water, paints, clay and other potential irritants.

- Most pupils with eczema cannot tolerate synthetic fibres. 100% cotton clothing is often recommended wherever possible. This may have implications for dressing-up activities.

- Synthetic cotton wool may cause irritation for some pupils. Note: Cotton wool is frequently used in Christmas decorations and similar materials are used for stuffing toys.

- Soap is an irritant for many pupils and is usually best avoided.

- Pupils should be kept on task to minimise opportunities for scratching, as this can lead to bleeding sores if unchecked. Concentration can be affected.

- Consideration should be given to the pupil's position in the classroom if he/she reacts to sunlight and excessive dust.

- The classroom should be well ventilated and pupils should be encouraged to remove layers of top clothing if the classroom is warm.

- Pupils may find that their pencil grip is affected if their hands are badly affected by the eczema. A fat pencil or a pencil grip can help.

- Chlorinated water causes problems for many pupils. Barrier cream may be required before swimming. Showering and application of cream is likely to be required afterwards.

Epilepsy

Definition

Epilepsy is defined as *"a condition in which there is a tendency for a person to experience recurring epileptic seizures over a period of time."* (Walker & Shorvon[1]). Seizures are a symptom of the condition, and the type of seizure experienced indicates the area of the brain affected.

- Epilepsy affects 1 in 133 of the UK population.
- In 75–80% of cases it can be controlled by medication.
- Most of those with childhood epilepsy will grow out of it.

Causes

Whether an individual develops epilepsy depends on two factors, their inherited threshold level (primary epilepsy) and life circumstances (secondary epilepsy). Any of the causes below would come under the heading of 'life circumstances':

- brain damage due to a difficult birth;
- a severe blow to the head;
- a stroke which starves the brain of oxygen;
- blood chemical abnormalities, e.g. low calcium, magnesium or glucose;
- an infection of the brain, such as meningitis;
- very rarely, a brain tumour.

Seizures fall into two groups – either generalised seizures occurring across the whole brain, or partial seizures affecting one area only.

Types of seizures

- **Childhood absence seizures**, (previously known as 'petit mal'), which are the most common form of childhood epilepsy.
- **Tonic-clonic**, (previously known as 'grand mal'). This is the classic seizure of which most people are aware in which the pupil loses consciousness.
- **Benign Rolandic seizures**, (previously known as 'simple partial seizures'), which are confined to one area of the brain and consciousness may or may not be lost.
- **Complex partial seizures** during which the pupil either loses consciousness completely or becomes vague, looks dazed and does not respond when spoken to.
- **Atonic drop attacks** (rare) during which there is a sudden loss of muscle tone and the pupil falls to the ground.
- **Myoclonic seizures** (also rare) – similar to atonic drop attacks but differing in that there is a sudden muscle 'jerk' after which the pupil falls to the ground.

1 'Understanding Epilepsy' by Dr M. Walker & Professor S. Shorvon (BMA) Family Doctor Series 1996

- **'Status epilepticus'** is when a seizure lasts for more than the usual length of time (approximately 5–10 minutes) or if the pupil has recurrent seizures one after another. Follow the emergency procedure which forms part of the pupil's individual health care plan (IHCP).

Possible triggers of seizures

- forgotten or incorrect medication;
- illness/high temperature;
- lack of sleep or food;
- emotional stress;
- excitement/boredom;
- flashing lights (very rare, 3–5% only);
- changes in hormone levels;
- drugs/alcohol.

Long-term treatment

Effective seizure control is gained in 75–80% of those with epilepsy by the following means:

i) avoidance of all known seizure 'triggers';

ii) medication (this is monitored by feedback from parents and school staff);

iii) brain surgery (very rare).

For further information contact:

Epilepsy Action
Anstey House, 40 Hanover Square
Leeds L53 1BE
Helpline 0808 800 5050 or Email helpline at <www.epilepsy.org.uk

David Lewis Centre
Alderley Edge
Mobberley
Cheshire SK9 7UD

Tel: 0156 587 2613

www.davidlewis.org.uk

National Society for Epilepsy
Chalfont Society for Epilepsy
Chalfont St Peter
Buckinghamshire SL9 0RJ

Tel: 01494 601400

www.epilepsynse.org.uk

Educational implications (epilepsy)

Put into context, the incidence of one in 133 of the UK population having epilepsy, means that in a medium-sized primary school, (300 on roll) two pupils will be affected and in a large primary school, (600 on roll) four pupils will have the condition.

Every school should therefore be familiar with the condition of epilepsy and plan to meet the individual needs of each pupil. The head teacher and governing body need to:

- develop a 'Whole School Policy' to meet the needs of pupils with epilepsy;
- raise awareness of the condition amongst staff through INSET and ensure that all staff are familiar with the management of Tonic-Clonic seizures in school;
- nominate staff to administer drugs – N.B. this must be on a voluntary basis;
- arrange for the training of nominated staff;
- identify an easily accessible area for storage and administration of drugs;
- keep accurate records of seizures occurring and pass on to parents;
- monitor changes in mood, behaviour, learning;
- share relevant information with staff bearing in mind issues of confidentiality;
- identify 'at risk' factors (e.g. triggers of seizures) for an individual pupil.

General school organisational issues

Anti-epileptic medication gives 75-80% of pupils the opportunity to lead normal lives. However the following are considerations which apply to the remaining 20–25% of pupils.

- Ensure that new staff are made aware of the school policy.
- Timetable lessons on the ground floor if possible, for safety reasons.
- Certain subjects, namely science, food technology, PE and some elements of art, will involve safety issues.
- Assess the need for adult supervision during movement between classes or break times.
- Encourage peer support and empathy through Personal, Social and Health Education (PSHE).
- Encourage the development of a whole-life ethos to reduce the incidence and consequences of seizures, e.g. learning to pace themselves etc.
- Include pupils in school outings and residential visits, ensuring adequate supervision and careful planning.
- Likewise, pupils should participate in sports wherever possible following advice regarding safety.

Specific advice

Tiredness and lethargy:

- Encourage parents to pass on information regarding nocturnal seizures (home/ school book);
- note the problem and possible learning missed and keep records to pass on to consultant/parents;
- provide differentiated work if appropriate.

Photosensitivity:

- for the 3–5% of those who fall into this group care will need to be taken when using computers, e.g. fit a glare screen if necessary, take regular breaks away from the screen (Health & Safety Guidelines);
- sit the pupil in the shade in a sunny classroom;
- ensure they wear sunglasses outside during the summer.

Teaching implications of epilepsy

Be aware that:

- the type, frequency and duration of seizure;
- the original cause, (i.e. brain damage) and area of the brain involved; and
- poor self-image, social factors and side effects from medication

may impact on:

- learning;
- concentration;
- memory;
- behaviour;
- language and communication skills;
- fine and gross motor skills;
- self-esteem.

For more detailed information about the effects of epilepsy on learning, consult the book in the same series 'Supporting Pupils with Epilepsy' and the section on strategies in Sections 2–4 of this book.

Haemophilia

Definition and cause

Haemophilia is a group of blood disorders in which there is a defect in the blood clotting mechanism. Haemophilia is a lifelong, inherited genetic condition affecting people from all races. The clotting factors in normal blood are numbered from I to XIII. There are two main types of haemophilia:

Haemophilia A (classic haemophilia) is when Factor VIII is defective.

Haemophilia B is when Factor IX is defective.

- Only males are affected with Haemophilia A and B although females are the carriers.
- The condition varies from mild to severe.
- Severe haemophilia is characterised by frequent and spontaneous bleeding into joints, particularly knees, ankles and elbows, causing inflammation, swelling and pain.
- Bleeding into muscles may occur as a result of a knock or fall.
- Cuts and scratches should stop bleeding as with any other pupil.

Treatment

- Injecting Coagulation Factor Concentrate treats severe haemophilia bleeding episodes. A single injection usually controls a bleed.
- 'Home treatment' is usually appropriate for simple bleeds. Parents can be trained to inject concentrate and pupils can also learn to self-inject.
- The joint should be rested after treatment for a bleed.
- Prophylactic therapy (a preventative treatment) can be used, particularly with children. This is when Coagulation Factor Concentrate is infused two or three times a week, in order to prevent joint bleeds. This is often administered through an in-dwelling device 'Port-a-cath' which delivers the medication directly into the vein.

For further information contact:

Haemophilia Society
Chesterfield House
385 Euston Road
London NW1 3AU

Tel: 020 7380 0600
www.haemophilia.org.uk

Educational implications (haemophilia)

Pupils with haemophilia bruise easily. However, it is a misconception that they bleed excessively from normal cuts and grazes. Spontaneous internal bleeding into the joints, muscles and other parts of the body can occur. Pupils generally recognise the "feel" of internal bleeding before external signs such as bruising and swelling are visible. It is therefore essential that staff listen to a pupil if he reports these "feelings". Several points should be considered prior to admitting a pupil to school. A health care plan should be written ensuring that the following are included:

1. what constitutes an emergency for this pupil;

2. what procedures should be followed if a pupil feels a 'bleed';

3. emergency contacts in case parents/guardians are unavailable.

The health care plan should be drawn up in consultation with the parents and a medical practitioner such as the haemophilia support nurse.

- Health and Safety policy regarding handling bodily fluids. There should be clear guidelines regarding handling of bodily fluids, provision of hygiene requisites such as gloves, and disposal and cleaning routines. DfEE advice suggests all bodily fluids should be handled as though there were a possibility of HIV transmission.

- Awareness raising – relevant staff, volunteers and pupils should be aware of the guidelines for dealing with spillage of blood (and other bodily fluid).

- Confidentiality – the pupil's full medical history should not be disclosed without permission, to protect his or her privacy under the Human Rights Act. Issues such as Hepatitis, HIV and AIDS can cause undue prejudice and/or hysteria in a school community. If these conditions are disclosed by a pupil, parent or health care worker they should be dealt with in strict confidence and with sensitivity.

- Mobility support may be required following 'bleeds' which result in swelling or pain.

- Planning for out-of-school activities would include all the above points.

- Additional support or alternative activities in P.E. lessons may be required. Sporting activities can be categorised as low/medium/or high risk according to level of exertion, need for protective gear and potential for contact with other pupils.

Low/medium risk	Medium risk	High risk
Swimming	Rounders	Football at senior level
Dancing	Cricket	Rugby at senior level
Sailing	Baseball	Hockey
Athletics, cycling	Motor cross/motor cycle	Judo at training level
Skiing		Wrestling, boxing
Soccer, baseball		
Racquet sports		

First aid procedures (pupils with haemophilia)

> **Remember:**
> - wear gloves for any open bleeding;
> - clean up blood spills using 10% bleach solution and paper towels – dispose of in a strong plastic bag, via the clinical waste disposal service or by incineration.

Cuts and abrasions

Small cuts, scrapes and bruises do not usually cause problems. Cover with a plaster or dressing, apply pressure and elevate if necessary. Deep cuts that need stitching will require treatment at the haemophilia centre.

Nose bleeds

Apply pressure to the nostril for 10–20 minutes or apply an ice pack to the bridge of the nose for no more than 5 minutes.

Mouth and tongue bleeds

These can be hard to control because blood clots are washed away by saliva or by food. Try giving the pupil an ice cube or an ice lolly to suck. Treatment at the haemophilia centre will be required if the bleeding does not stop.

Joint bleeds

Main signs of internal bleeding are pain or a 'funny feeling', swelling, warmth of the skin at the site of the internal bleed, loss of movement in the joint or muscle. Younger pupils may not recognise these signs: watch for the pupil protecting a joint by limping or not using it and treat as soon as possible at the haemophilia centre.

Face, neck and throat injuries

These must be treated promptly by parents or the haemophilia centre.

Head injury

a) **Bumps to the head** – if the pupil is not distressed or in pain, the bump is not likely to have caused any problems. If in doubt send for treatment. As with all head injuries *inform parents so that the pupil can be observed for 12 hours.*

b) **Minor head injuries** – bumps that lead to bruising and small cuts should always be treated either by the parents or the haemophilia centre. As with all head injuries *inform parents so that the pupil can be observed for 12 hours.*

c) **Serious injuries** – if the pupil receives a heavy blow to the head or is unconscious, the injury should be treated as soon as possible at the haemophilia centre.

Signs to watch for:

- persistent or increasing headaches;
- vomiting;
- sleepiness or a change in behaviour;
- weakness/clumsiness in arm/leg;
- stiffness or pain in the pupil's neck;
- blurred/double vision, crossed eyes;
- poor balance;
- fits or convulsions.

Head injury, accidents, meningitis, brain tumour, stroke

Definition

A head injury is any kind of injury to the head and/or the brain. The brain is a dense mass of nerve tissue. It rests on the base of the skull, surrounded and bathed by cerebrospinal fluid.

Injury, either by accident, infection, stroke, or brain tumour might result in loss of function in one or more areas of the brain, due to damaged or torn nerve tissue and/or blood vessels.

Causes

Accidents, including road traffic accidents (RTAs)

- In any accident the extent of the injury depends on the severity and type of accident, e.g. fall, impact, or blow to the head.
- Road traffic accidents are the most common cause of severe head injury in children.
- In these cases impact to the head results in injury, both at the site of the blow and to the area directly opposite, as the brain rebounds off the inside of the skull (similar to injury resulting from shaking).
- Initial damage might range from:
    - superficial bruising or cuts;
    - skull fracture;
    - subdural haematoma (a blood clot between the skull and the surface of the brain) at the site of the blow;
    - to possible loss of consciousness.
- Complications may follow owing to bruising and swelling of the brain, causing increased pressure within the skull. Pressure is put on blood vessels, cutting off oxygen to the nerve cells, and on the brain stem (at the base of the brain) which regulates breathing, heart beat etc.
- If an object penetrates the skull and brain there might be consequent neurological infections.
- Depending on the area of the brain injured, paralysis, impaired vision or memory, and possibly onset of epilepsy may be short-term, or long-term, consequences. Post-traumatic loss of memory is also common.

Meningitis

- This condition is the result of viral or bacterial infection causing inflammation of the meninges, the membranes which cover the surface of the brain and spinal cord.

- Eighty percent of cases are seen in children under 15 years of age and most of these occur in the under-fives.

- The most serious form is bacterial meningitis. Types include pneumococcal, streptococcal, and the most common haemophilus influenza type B. This is the cause of meningitis in the 1–4 year age range.

Recognising meningitis

- Symptoms of *viral meningitis* include headache (worse on bending), fever, nausea and vomiting, and a stiff neck. In more severe cases there might be muscle weakness, paralysis, impaired speech or double vision.

- Symptoms of *bacterial meningitis* include any of the above, but also a rash of red spots, drowsiness and eventual coma.

- If meningitis is suspected, call for medical assistance as quickly as possible.

- Hospital treatment is usually a lumbar puncture (to test cerebrospinal fluid). If meningitis is confirmed, massive doses of antibiotics are given, together with fluids to prevent dehydration. It might also be necessary to use a ventilator to aid breathing, due to pressure on the brain stem.

- Vaccinations help prevent the spread of infection.

Brain tumour

- Cells die and are replaced constantly. Occasionally the blueprint for a cell will go wrong and the 'wrong' pattern reproduces itself again and again causing a 'tumour'. These can be either benign (non-cancerous) or malignant (cancerous).

- Possible treatment of a malignant tumour might be surgical removal, chemotherapy, or radiotherapy that is carefully targeted to kill the cells.

- Benign tumours are usually surgically removed.

- Epilepsy is a common consequence of a brain tumour, owing to the invasive nature of such growths.

Stroke

- A stroke is the result of a blood clot blocking a small artery or blood vessel. This cuts off oxygen to that area of the brain, killing nerve cells. Additional damage may be caused by brain swelling.

- Hospital treatment consists of medication to reduce brain swelling and the possible use of a ventilator to assist breathing if pressure is put on the brain stem.

- The resulting difficulties depends on the area in which the stroke occurred and the extent of the damage to nerve cells.

- The most common symptoms of stroke are paralysis or numbness down one side of the body, dizziness and loss of balance, speech difficulties and visual impairment.

- These can be long or short term depending on how quickly treatment was begun and the recuperative abilities of the brain.

- Although rare, very young children may have a stroke. Recuperation is generally better than for adults with good long-term prognosis.

Treatment of head injury following an accident in school

- If the injury occurs in school, follow the normal first aid procedure and seek medical advice if necessary.

- Be aware that a lack of external injury to the head does not always indicate the extent of damage to the brain.

- Always monitor the pupil for any after effects, particularly concussion (i.e. tiredness or nausea), difficulties with swallowing or coughing for no reason. Seek medical advice as soon as possible.

- For more serious accidents, resulting in loss of consciousness, do not move the pupil unless he/she is at further risk of injury. Keep the pupil warm, place in the recovery position and check that the airway is clear.

- Call the emergency services immediately and inform parents.

Hospital treatment

At the hospital medical treatment may include skull X-rays and/or a brain scan, medication to reduce swelling, or surgery to remove blood clots.

Occasionally, pressure on the brain stem causes breathing difficulties and a ventilator is needed to aid breathing.

For further information contact:

Headway
The Nat Head Injuries Assoc Ltd
7 King Edward Court, King Edward St
Nottingham NG1 1EW
Tel: 0115 924 0800

HIRE (Head Injury Re-Education)
Portland College
Nottingham Rd
Mansfield
Nottingham NG18 4TJ
www.stroke.org

Meningitis Research Foundation
Midland Way, Thornbury
Bristol BS35 2BS

The British Brain Tumour Assoc
2 Oakfield Road
Hightown
Merseyside L38 9GQ
Tel: 0151 929 3229

The Stroke Association
Stroke House
Whitecross Street
London EC1Y 8JJ
Tel: 020 7566 0300
Helpline: 0843 3033 100

Educational implications (head injuries)

By the time a pupil who has sustained a head injury is ready to return to school, he/she will be in the recovery phase, which may or may not last for many months. It is difficult to generalise advice for pupils returning to school following a head injury, as the degree of difficulty can vary enormously according to the age of the pupil and the area and extent of damage.

The difficulties experienced by those pupils whose injuries have resulted in severe physical disabilities, are likely to be obvious, in that they are visible. For example:

- mobility problems;
- paralysis or loss of function in a limb.

Other difficulties may not be so easy to detect, but may also have a significant impact on the pupil's ability to access the curriculum. For example:

- visual impairment;
- speech or hearing difficulties;
- epilepsy;
- short and long term memory problems;
- reduced stamina;
- emotional and behavioural problems.

It is essential that schools be given as much information as possible about the pupil's condition, prior to his/her return, so that appropriate strategies can be put in place.

Refer to the following sections for possible strategies to deal with the following issues:

- accessing the building;
- accessing the curriculum;
- alternative recording strategies;
- supporting short-term memory problems;
- developing organisational skills;
- developing concentration skills/promoting listening skills;
- developing visual perception;
- developing self-esteem;
- promoting positive peer group relationships;
- emotional issues.

Refer to *Supporting Children with Epilepsy* and *Supporting Children with Behavioural Difficulties* from the same series for advice about epilepsy, resulting from a brain tumour and consequent behaviour issues.

Heart conditions (congenital)

Definition

This is the term given to abnormalities of the heart at birth. They affect approximately 1:100 births.

Cause

It is sometimes difficult to determine the cause of the problem. Children's heart conditions usually develop during pregnancy; in some cases the problems may be genetic. The underlying problem, however, whatever the cause, is the abnormal development of the heart.

Listed below are the most common types of heart condition affecting children:

- *Aortic Stenosis* describes how the aortic valve, situated between the aorta and left ventricle, is very narrow. This causes the heart to be stressed, since the pumping of blood has to cope with a small area, making the heart work harder. This condition is usually detected during normal medical checks. Symptoms may include dizziness, chest pain or loss of consciousness.

- *Atrial Septal Defect* describes a hole between the left and right atrium; there are often no symptoms in childhood and there may be gradual damage to the heart muscle.

- *Pulmonary Atresia* describes the absence of a valve and often an absence of the pulmonary artery between the lungs and right ventricle. It results in a complete blockage and the child presents as a blue baby.

- *Coarctation of the Aorta* describes part of the aorta as being very narrow, thus impeding the flow of blood to other areas in the body. Babies usually require surgery. In older children symptoms can include tiredness, cramps, heart murmur, and high blood pressure in the arms and a weak pulse in the legs.

Heart murmurs

Although a heart murmur is not a particular illness, it indicates that there is some irregularity in the passage of deoxygenated blood, which should return via the veins to the heart. The word murmur describes a "swishing" sound in the blood. Heart murmurs may not be detected until the child is about 2 or 3 years old, as the child has to be calm and quiet for the detection of this condition, which is difficult to hear.

Overweight and heart disease risk

The problems connected with overweight include high cholesterol, diabetes and especially heart disease. This in turn, causes breathlessness, movement difficulties and the possibility of more serious repercussions. In consultation with the GP, it is possible to recommend safe diets for overweight children. An exercise regime may also be recommended to manage weight problems. This must be at all times in consultation with the child's doctor.

Treatment

Treatment of heart conditions can include surgery or a series of operations which will either improve function or correct the abnormality.

For further information contact:

British Heart Foundation
14 Fitzhardinge Street
London W1H 4DH

www.bhf.org.uk

Contact A Family
209–211 City Road
London EC1V 1JW

Tel: 020 7608 8700
Helpline: 0808 808 3555

www.caf.org.uk

Children's Heart Foundation
0808 808 5000
Mon–Fri 9.30 a.m. to 9.30 p.m.

www.childrens-heart-fed.org.uk

Educational implications (heart conditions)

Many pupils with congenital heart conditions are able to be self-limiting within school and therefore manage their condition independently. Generally, cognitive ability is not affected by the heart condition. However, staff should be aware that lack of concentration could be associated with a decrease in arterial oxygen concentration, which is most likely to occur after physical exertion.

There are some pupils who require a variety of support arrangements according to their individual need. These may include:

- placement of tutor group, room allocation, timetabling issues, with reference to frequency of climbing stairs;

- additional adult support to monitor and assist with movement around school and transportation of belongings;

- provision of an additional set of textbooks to minimise the volume of books to be carried to and from school;

- storage facilities for personal belongings to reduce the weight of the school bag;

- additional support in design and technology and practical science lessons, to minimise physical demands of the lesson: masks may be required in D&T to prevent inhalation of dust: in addition, the pupil may have to avoid science experiments that involve fumes and/or smoke;

- alternative activities during PE lessons, to enable the pupil to follow replacement programmes of study;

- suitable furniture, (e.g. perching stools), to take account of the effect of prolonged standing in practical lessons;

- a stair climber or lift may be required to allow access to upstairs classrooms;

- a wheelchair that is compatible with the stair climber may be required for mobility around school when necessary;

- a small trolley to use in the dining room;

- access to home tuition may be required following surgery, or during prolonged periods of absence;

- accurate sharing of information about the pupil's condition to all staff;

- flexibility by staff regarding the timescale for completion of homework, due to fatigue;

- arrangements to allow the pupil to maintain fluid intake during or between lessons, without asking permission, if this is required;

- arrangements for the pupil to remain inside at breaks and lunchtimes during inclement weather;

- establishment of appropriate monitoring and liaison strategies with continuity of additional adult support to enable careful monitoring of the pupil's condition and regular liaison with parents, if necessary;

- careful positioning within the classroom, as the pupil may need to avoid sitting in direct sunlight. Classrooms should be well ventilated;

- awareness of the need for the pupil to be as independent as possible.

Hip problems

Definition

Developmental dysplasia of the hip (DDH) describes a variety of conditions in which the ball and socket of the hip do not develop properly. In the mildest forms, the socket may fail to grow deeply enough. In the more severe forms, the femoral head or ball may be displaced completely out of the socket and be dislocated.

Causes

Although there are no definite causes of hip problems such as DDH, there are a number of factors that may be relevant to the disorder.

- breech birth or breech position in the last three months of pregnancy;
- a family history of hip problems or double jointedness;
- lack of fluid surrounding the baby in the womb (oligohydramnios);
- the increase in maternal hormones before delivery may make the susceptible baby's hip more likely to displace at the time of birth;
- wrapping a baby's legs too tightly after birth;
- girls are more often affected than boys, particularly the first born;
- hip problems are more common in babies who have mild foot deformities or tightness in the neck.

Treatment

If the condition is detected around the time of birth, a lightweight splint which holds the legs apart (abducted) may be applied. The splint is worn for several weeks and is only removed at the clinic. Some children do not respond to early treatment while others are not detected until they are older. The approach to treatment for this group is slightly different, and a number of treatment options are available:

- admission to hospital for X-rays and a short period of traction;
- a small operation in the groin area under a general anaesthetic;
- a more extensive operation to put the ball and socket in place.

It is normal to put the child in a plaster of paris/fibre glass cast known as a hip spica. Treatment in plaster will continue for several weeks or months and may be followed by a period in a splint. After a short stay in hospital most children return home with visits to the Outpatient Clinic for check-ups. Some children may return to school in a hip spica.

The prognosis is generally good when diagnosed early and treated accordingly, although normal mobility may be delayed. There is also a tendency towards arthritis later on, with additional complications such as irritable skin or slight inequalities of leg length.

> *For further information contact:*
> http://steps-charity.org.uk/hip problems

Educational implications (hip problems)

Advice is usually available from the orthopaedic department or the physiotherapy department involved in the care of pupils with these conditions. The majority of children are diagnosed in infancy and with successful treatment will not present with difficulties in school. A few pupils, however, may have residual pain and/or limited mobility, following late diagnosis, treatment, and during the rehabilitation period.

The following are general considerations:

- Symptoms of joint pain and stiffness can vary from day to day.

- Rest is recommended for severe pain, some pupils require analgesia (pain killers) in school. Rest is best done at home if pain is severe.

- Restricted mobility may, in some cases, require use of a wheelchair over long distances. It is not usually necessary for pupils to stay in their wheelchairs within the classroom. This may have an impact on out-of-school visits and school transport arrangements.

- Pupils may have difficulty sitting on the floor during carpet time and assemblies.

- Prolonged sitting in examinations can contribute to discomfort. Additional rest breaks can be requested through the examinations officer.

- Low-impact exercise, walking, swimming, cycling, is very good for pupils with these conditions. High-impact sports and contact sports should be avoided.

- Pupils can generally be relied upon to be self-limiting in physical activities.

- Long absences from school are possible following orthopaedic surgery. In a minority of cases home tuition may be recommended.

- In rare instances, pupils may need to return to school whilst in hip spica or broomstick plasters. In these instances the Special Educational Needs section at the LEA should be involved, if additional support is required for toileting, mobility and transport issues.

- Close liaison between the family, health professionals and other relevant outside agencies will ensure changing needs can be met.

Hirschsprung's disease

Definition

Hirschsprung's disease is a serious childhood condition, which occurs once in 5,000 births. It is a genetic disorder, which results in a lack of spontaneous bowel movements, which can lead to chronic constipation and/or diarrhoea, vomiting, lack of appetite and abdominal distension.

Cause

Children born with this condition have an absence of nerve cells (ganglion cells) in portions of the bowel wall. The ganglion cells are responsible for co-ordinating the relaxation of the muscles in the bowel wall, which allows stools to pass along. Where there is an absence of ganglion cells, the bowel remains collapsed and stools cannot pass.

Treatment

It is usual for the affected portion of bowel to be surgically removed and the healthy sections rejoined. A single procedure known as a "pull through" operation is frequently performed. This is where the affected portion of the bowel is removed and the healthy bowel is joined to the rectal wall. Sometimes a colostomy is required prior to this operation if the child is too small or too ill. The colostomy operation involves bringing the colon out to the surface of the abdomen through a surgically formed hole called a stoma, so that the stools can be discharged into a special pouch for disposal.

Most children have no long-term complications after successful surgery to repair the bowel. However, there is a significant minority of children who continue to experience constipation, encopresis (stool incontinence) or persistent enterocolitis (inflammation of the large and small intestine).

For further information contact:
Gut Motility Support Network
7 Walden Road
Sewards End
Saffron Walden CB10 2LE

http://www.aboutkidsgi.org/hirchsprungs.html

Some pupils who have Hirschsprung's disease are likely to have periods of bowel incontinence during their time at school. For some pupils the emphasis, therefore, must be placed on independent management of their bowel incontinence rather than toilet training. It is likely that a pupil with Hirschsprung's disease will experience leakage of fluid matter rather than solid faeces. Some pupils will be oblivious to, or will deny the existence of the odour, whereas other pupils will be highly sensitive to the possibility that classmates will detect an odour.

Consider the following points:

- sensitive sharing of information regarding the condition, with relevant staff;
- access to a private toilet facility with waste disposal and washing facilities;
- arrangements to enable the pupil to leave the classroom discreetly when necessary;
- arrangements to ensure a supply of clean underwear and wet wipes are available;
- access to drinks, as a regular fluid intake is usually recommended.

Self-management in early years (see section 2 for detailed strategies)

The emphasis should be placed on establishing a routine where the pupil checks his/her nappy/trainer pants/underwear for signs of soiling, at regular intervals, with adult support. Additional visits to the toilet will be required to deal with soiling incidents identified by smell.

Self-management in key stage 1 (see section 2 for detailed strategies)

Building on the work done in Early Years the pupil will be encouraged to initiate visits to the toilet at regular intervals. He/she should be encouraged to take responsibility for as much of the cleansing and changing routine as is possible.

Self-management in key stage 2 (see section 2 for detailed strategies)

The pupil should now be encouraged to implement his/her cleansing and changing routine independently with oversight for emotional support and guidance. It is hoped that independence will have been achieved well before secondary school transfer.

Self-management in key stages 3 & 4 (see section 2 for detailed strategies)

Pupils generally manage their own cleansing and changing routines at KS3/4. It is essential that staff are sensitive to the pupil's need for privacy. Some pupils have difficulties around the time of puberty and can begin to deny that they have a problem. This may result in peer pressure.

Hydrocephalus

Definition

The Association for Spina Bifida and Hydrocephalus (ASBAH) gives the following information about the types and causes of Hydrocephalus:

'Hydrocephalus is commonly known as "water on the brain". A watery fluid known as cerebro-spinal fluid (CSF) is produced inside the brain. The CSF normally flows through narrow pathways from one ventricle to the next, then out over the outside of the brain and down the spinal cord.

If the drainage pathways are blocked at any point, the fluid accumulates in the ventricles inside the brain, causing them to swell. In babies and infants, the head will enlarge. In older children and adults, the head size cannot increase as the bones which form the skull are completely joined together.'

Cause

Hydrocephalus is caused by the inability of CSF to drain away into the bloodstream. There are many reasons why this can happen:

- Congenital Hydrocephalus
- Spina Bifida
- Brain Haemorrhage
- Cysts within the brain
- Prematurity
- Normal pressure (Late onset) Hydrocephalus
- Meningitis
- Tumours Genetic

Treatment

Some forms of hydrocephalus do not need any treatment. Some types of hydrocephalus require surgery. This usually involves inserting a shunting device to drain the excess cerebro-spinal fluid, thus preventing a deterioration of the condition. The shunt does not cure the condition; it does however, control it. The symptoms which were caused by raised pressure do normally improve; however other problems can still remain.

> *For further information contact:*
> ASBAH
> 42 Park Road
> Peterborough PE1 2UG
>
> Tel: 01733 555988
> www.asbah.org

Educational implications (hydrocephalus)

Not all pupils with hydrocephalus will have learning difficulties: ability levels range from severe learning difficulties to above average ability. It is therefore important that staff do not have pre-conceived ideas about an individual pupil's ability. Pupils of average ability who have hydrocephalus may appear to have more problems than their peers in:

- focusing on their work;
- thinking and working independently;
- assessing the standard of their own work.

In addition some pupils with hydrocephalus may have:

Poor short-term memory

- struggles to remember instructions;
- has difficulty taking part in class discussions and listening to stories;
- has difficulty remembering facts e.g. addition facts and multiplication tables;
- has problems acquiring reading and spelling skills.

Short attention span

- is easily distracted by external stimuli.

Faulty spatial awareness and visual perceptual deficits

- difficulty in judging distances – bumps into furniture, walls, misses targets;
- poor sense of direction.

Spatial and perceptual difficulties are most frequently observed in the following areas:

PE

- off-the-floor activities;
- field activities;
- target activities.

Presentation skills

- setting out work/writing on lines;
- drawing and completing tables/charts;
- copying from the board.

Maths

- may find algebra difficult because of problems recognising patterns;
- will find spatial relationships and symmetry difficult;
- will have difficulty sorting objects.

Practical lessons

- handling tools safely, e.g. cutting along a line, judging distances between containers when pouring fluids.

Lack of motivation and initiation

- may sit and wait for individual instructions rather than follow class instructions;
- needs verbal prompts to start work;
- may have difficulty participating in class discussions.

Inability to generalise

- has difficulty taking concepts learned in one area and applying them to another;
- may require frequent and deliberate over-learning;
- may not realise that a reprimand has been given to a group of pupils.

Difficulty understanding inference, takes everything very literally

- for example, a teacher might say to the class, "Wake up!"... the pupil with hydrocephalus might respond, "I'm not asleep."

Sequencing difficulties/poor organisational skills

- appears to be poorly organised in thought and action (links with memory problems).

Poor concept of time

- no inclination to hurry;
- five minutes can seem the same as an hour.

Poor hand function

- many pupils with hydrocephalus have weak hand skills similar to dyspraxia;
- many pupils find neat handwriting impossible to achieve: if neat handwriting is not achieved prior to the end of KS2, it is unlikely to improve drastically.

Classroom observations and teacher assessment will identify strengths and weaknesses and will inform the individual education plan (IEP). Pupils may require educational targets and or physical targets.

Health care considerations for pupils with hydrocephalus

Many pupils with hydrocephalus have a shunt fitted. Blockage of a shunt will result in raised pressure within the brain and can have serious consequences if undetected. School staff need to be aware that the following symptoms could indicate a problem:

- sudden or recurring headaches;
- vomiting;
- seizures;
- raised temperature;
- unusual listlessness and apathy;
- change or deterioration in vision.

An individual health care plan is required to outline the medical condition, state what constitutes an emergency for this pupil and what procedures to follow.

Hypermobility syndromes

Hypermobility describes over-flexibility of the joints. Hypermobility syndromes refer to a family of conditions which have over-flexible joints in common, although the cause and degree of involvement may be different. Additionally individual members of a family may be affected to a greater or lesser degree.

All the conditions involve problems with the supporting tissues of the body, i.e. ligaments, tendons, joints and muscle, due to faulty proteins in the connective tissue that would normally act as 'glue' and give the body its strength. Individuals with these conditions inherit looser and more brittle connective tissue; consequently lax joints may result in injury through over-use, or dislocation. Pain is a common symptom of the condition.

It is estimated that 7–10% of children have loose joints and occasional pain ('growing pains'). Most grow out of it as joints become stronger.

Benign joint hypermobility syndrome (BJHS)

This lies at the mild end of the hypermobility continuum and is autosomal dominant, i.e. 50% of the offspring will carry the gene for the condition. The abnormal protein for this condition is collagen Type 1 (the most common). Some individuals show little evidence of joint problems.

Ehlers-Danlos syndrome (EDS)

Ehlers-Danlos syndrome is made up of a large group of conditions that has now been reduced to six major subtypes, which are classified and diagnosed by their individual symptoms. Ehlers-Danlos Hypermobile Type (formerly EDS III) and BJHS are now considered to be the same condition. EDS is inherited in a variety of ways, mostly by a dominant gene from either parent, while other forms may require a recessive gene from both parents. Occasionally it is linked to the X chromosome, which causes the condition in boys. 'Types' tend to run true for each family.

Prevalence is between 1 in 5,000 and 1 in 10,000.

In addition to having hypermobile joints, individuals with EDS also have differences in skin texture. Joint problems range from:

- hyperextensible joints (i.e. they move beyond the normal range of movement); to
- lax joints which are liable to dislocate.

Skin fragility might show itself in:

- soft and velvety skin;
- more elastic skin which tears or bruises easily;
- slow and poor healing of wounds;
- development of pseudotumours (fleshy lesions over scar or pressure areas).

Less common problems associated with some types of EDS are arterial/intestine/uterine fragility, scoliosis, mitral valve prolapse and gum disease.

Diagnosis is based on family history and clinical findings.

Treatment

- By teaching joint protection through careful management of physical activities.
- Sometimes joints may require splinting to improve support, e.g. the ankles.
- Skin care is again by teaching self management to protect skin, e.g. using sun block or covering up during sunny weather.

Marfan syndrome

This lies at the more severe end of the continuum. In this condition the disorder of the connective tissue is the result of a genetic defect affecting the body's production of fibrillin, a protein that is the main component of microfibrils. These allow tissues to stretch repeatedly without weakening. Mostly the condition runs in families, inherited by an autosomal dominant gene, although in 25% of cases it results from a spontaneous mutation on chromosome 15.

Prevalence is between 1 in 3,000 and 1 in 5,000 of the population.

Individuals are typically tall and thin with disproportionately long arms and legs, fingers and toes. The disorder affects three systems of the body:

- bones and muscles;
- the heart and circulatory system;
- the eyes.

Bones are longer than usual, and ligaments weaker, therefore greater stress is placed on joints. Problems may be experienced in the following areas:

- the spine, e.g. scoliosis (sideways curves), kyphosis (outward curve) etc;
- inward curving sternum resulting in breathing difficulties;
- possible flat feet and/or frequent pain in the feet;
- hip problems.

Problems with the circulatory system result from the walls of blood vessels/heart being weaker and stretching more than usual. In particular the individual may have:

- aortic enlargement;
- aortic regurgitation (blood leaking back into the heart);
- a 'floppy' mitral valve (the valve between the chambers of the heart).

Eye problems range from myopia (short sight), dislocation of the lens, glaucoma or retinal detachment. Lungs can also be affected resulting in pneumothorax (collapse of a lung) and other chest conditions.

Diagnosis is based on family history and clinical findings.

Treatment

- Treatment is based on individual needs. Children are regularly checked for scoliosis of the spine; given an electrocardiogram (ECG) to check for heart problems, and eye checks.

- Pain in the feet can be treated with medication and sometimes individuals wear inserts in their shoes to support the feet.

Beals Syndrome (Beals arachnodactyly syndrome)

This is a rare genetic connective tissue disorder which is autosomal dominant. Individuals have:

- long, thin 'spider like' fingers and toes with congenital contractures of the fingers, hips, elbows, knees and ankles;

- scoliosis/kyphosis of the spine;

- crumpled ears;

- possible mitral valve prolapse.

Treatment is by surgery (to lengthen tendons), splints to support major joints, e.g. (ankles and feet, wrists etc). and input from the physical and occupational therapists to build muscle strength and, develop self-help (dressing, eating and toileting) strategies.

Useful contacts:

Contact a Family (CaF)
Helpline: 0808 808 3555
www.cafamily.org.uk

Ehlers-Danlos Syndrome
Support Group UK
PO Box 335, Surrey GU10 1XJ
www.atv.ndirect.co.uk

Nord (National Organisation of Rare Disorders)
www.rarediseases.org

Hypermobility Syndrome Association
15 Oakdene, Alton GU34 2AJ
www.hypermobility.org

Marfan Association
Rochester House
Rochester House
www.marfan.org.uk

Educational implications (hypermobility syndromes

The majority of pupils with these syndromes will require an individual health care plan to indicate areas of concern and strategies to overcome them. It would also help to look at the book in this series, *Supporting Children with Co-ordination Difficulties* since these pupils experience similar problems with low muscle tone. Whether a pupil is statemented will depend on the extent of his/her physical needs.

If there is a greater physical need pupils will be under the oversight of a physiotherapist and possibly an occupational therapist for joint care and to develop life skills. Often a physical management programme will be sent to the school and the therapist will visit on an arranged basis to review progress. Additional areas for consideration are as follows.

Access

Many pupils will have problems with access and may have difficulty:

- using stairs (use ramps or lifts instead);
- opening heavy doors or those with automatic closers adjust pressure to make it easier for pupils to open, or fit electro-magnetic door stops;
- negotiating a busy classroom, e.g. trip hazards.

Stamina

Stamina falls off dramatically as the day progresses. Staff should ensure that:

- parents send in high energy slow release snacks e.g. bananas, raisins, grain bars etc. for play breaks and ensure that the pupil has plenty of fluids;
- the pupil's wheelchair/buggy (if used) is sent in prior to outings/visits and if necessary a pre-visit has been made to look at wheelchair access.

Gross motor management/PE

Staff will need to ensure that the pupil does not:

- take part in rough and tumble play/activities;
- participate in contact games/sports;
- put undue pressure on joints e.g. running/jumping;
- over-exercise thereby causing damage to joints.

Fine motor skills

Pupils will usually have problems with fine motor activities owing to low muscle tone.

Skin care

- Consider the need for sun block on sunny days until the pupil is able to self monitor.
- If bruising occurs, use ice pack to reduce swelling and inform parents.

Juvenile arthritis

Definition

Juvenile arthritis (JA) is also known as juvenile rheumatoid arthritis and juvenile idiopathic arthritis. It is a condition which begins before the age of 16 and causes inflammation in one or more joints. The number of children known to have JA is 1 in 1,000. Juvenile arthritis may be difficult to diagnose because some children may not complain and joint swelling may not be immediately obvious. Limping, a reluctance to walk or a reluctance to use both hands may represent early signs. The condition can follow different patterns, which may require different treatments.

Systemic arthritis begins with a fever and rash and it is weeks or months before the arthritis is obvious.

Pauci-articular arthritis affects fewer than five joints and is the commonest form. It affects children under the age of five and girls are more affected by this type. It can be associated with eye problems (iritis). A large proportion of children with this type go into remission after three to four years, the remaining group progress to Polyarticular arthritis.

Polyarticular arthritis affects more than four joints, it begins at any age and girls are affected more than boys. The joints of the hands and feet are affected and pain, swelling and stiffness occurs. Problems with walking may result and difficulties with writing and manipulating equipment may be experienced. Children may feel unwell when the condition is active.

JA is a fluctuating condition so the pupil may function better on some days than others, some pupils may have stiff joints in the morning which improve as the day passes.

Causes

The precise cause of JA is as yet unknown. It is not thought to be directly inherited and it is rare for more than one family member to be affected.

Treatment

- Anti-inflammatory drugs can used to ease the condition.
- Physiotherapy and occupational therapy helps to reduce pain, increase joint function and prevent joint contractures.

For further information contact:
Children's Chronic Arthritis Association
Ground Floor Office
Amber Gate, City Walls Road
Worcester WR1 2AH

Tel: 01905 745595   www.ccaa.org.uk

Educational implications (juvenile arthritis)

Pupils with arthritis are usually under the care of a rheumatology consultant, who may recommend the involvement of a range of health professionals. Physiotherapy input would maintain joint mobility; occupational therapy advice may be given regarding daily living skills; an ophthalmologist may screen children with arthritis for iritis (a particular type of irritation); a podiatrist to provide foot orthoses. The following issues may need to be considered when planning to meet the educational needs of a pupil with arthritis:

- empowerment/independence – how the pupil will be enabled to be independent and make his/her own decisions;

- the fluctuating nature of the condition will result in good days and bad days;

- energy levels/motivation – a pupil who experiences constant or frequent pain can be debilitated and have depleted energy levels. Some youngsters may 'switch off';

- mobility – the pupil may be ambulant for some of the time and need a wheelchair or buggy for the rest. In more severe cases, a powered wheelchair may be required;

- fine motor adjustments – handwriting may be affected during flare-ups;

- furniture – a chair of an appropriate height and a tilting writing surface may be required, to prevent back and neck hunching;

- home tuition/catch-up strategies – frequent absences may be unavoidable;

- social/academic isolation can be the result of frequent absences, peer support through emails, text messages, letters and cards can help;

- home/school transport should be provided, if required;

- physical management routines – when, where, by whom;

- compliance – consider how to react if the pupil refuses to co-operate with physical management routines;

- self-care skills – restricted movement in joints may cause difficulty with personal hygiene routines. Where can the pupil receive discreet support?

- eyesight – be aware that redness of the eyes can be an early sign of iritis: monitor and mention to parents;

- restricted growth management implications (see section on restricted growth).

- joint protection issues will require further advice from the occupational therapist.

ME/CFS (chronic fatigue syndrome)

Definition

There are several different terms which describe this condition, the most commonly used are ME and CFS:

- ME or myalgic encephalopathy;
- CFS or chronic fatigue syndrome;
- PVFS or post-viral syndrome;
- CFIDS or chronic fatigue immune dysfunction syndrome.

Myalgic relates to muscular symptoms; encephalopathy relates to brain symptoms. Currently, there are approximately 150,000 people affected, of all ages and backgrounds. The common age range for the condition is mid teens to mid forties. The condition is rare in children under 7 or in people over 60. Females are a slightly higher risk group than men.

Cause

It must be noted that ME/CFS is a controversial subject; there is some scepticism and there is also some argument as to whether ME/CFS falls into either the category of psychiatric or physical causes. The World Health Organisation and The Royal College of Physicians now recognise the condition.

Common symptoms

- painful muscles;
- memory loss;
- disturbance in balance;
- constantly feeling unwell;
- sore throat;
- all common flu-like symptoms;
- serious fatigue;
- poor concentration;
- sleeping disorder;
- swollen glands;
- fluctuating temperature;
- depression.

Less common symptoms

- irritable bowel syndrome;
- allergic reactions.

Some effects

- disrupted education/employment;
- restricted social life;
- those most severely affected may be housebound or bedridden.

Treatment

There is no treatment for this condition, but there are a number of means by which the condition can be managed. These tend to include both medical and holistic alternative treatments:

- Low doses of sedative/anti-depressants for sleeping problems and muscular discomfort.

- Immunological treatments are tried with some patients.

- Non-chemical preparations such as Evening Primrose Oil.

- Acupuncture and homeopathic treatments may also help to alleviate symptoms.

The condition can also be managed with adjustments in lifestyle. In certain cases, there may be the need for periods of complete bed-rest. There is often a disruption to physical as well as mental activity. There may be the need for dietary adjustments, e.g. more carbohydrates to stabilise levels of blood sugar, less caffeine.

The recovery rate is both variable and unpredictable. It may be either short- or long-term. Sometimes recovery is only partial, with remissions and relapses. However, it is not generally thought to be a degenerative condition.

For further information contact:

The ME Association
4 Corrigan Road
Stanford-le-Hope
Essex SS17 0AH
Tel: 01375 642466

www.meassociation.org.uk

www.afme.org.uk

Educational implications (ME/CFS)

Pupils who have been diagnosed with Myalgic Encephalopathy (ME) or Chronic Fatigue Syndrome (CFS) are usually absent from school for a prolonged period, during the acute period of their illness. This is usually followed by a planned re-introduction to the school day. During the rehabilitation period, pupils have to learn how to live within their energy levels and carefully pace their activities, balancing physical and mental activity and rest.

- The pace of re-introduction is generally recommended by the consultant and supervised by the GP and/or the school doctor.

- Pupils who are severely affected will need home tuition until they are sufficiently recovered to begin a phased return to school.

- Some pupils may only be able to attend on a part-time basis.

- Others may continue at school with reduced activity particularly in PE and games.

- Assistance may be required with getting around the site, particularly in large secondary schools.

- Home/school transport may be required.

Muscular dystrophy

There are a number of different types of muscular dystrophy which share three common features: they are hereditary, progressive and each follows a characteristic pattern. The term dystrophy refers to a progressive weakness of the muscles due to a breakdown of the muscle fibre. At present there is no known cure for this group of conditions. Medical and surgical management along with physiotherapy and occupational therapy can improve the quality of life for children with these conditions.

The common forms of muscular dystrophy affecting children are:

- Duchenne muscular;
- Becker muscular dystrophy;
- Congenital myotonic dystrophy;
- Myotonic dystrophy;
- Spinal muscular atrophy.

Duchenne muscular dystrophy

This form of muscular dystrophy generally only affects boys. The condition may be diagnosed between the age of one and three when the child is unable to walk, run and jump like other children of his age. The child might struggle to get up from the floor and have difficulty climbing the stairs. Sometimes a diagnosis is not made until after the child starts school.

Between the ages of eight and eleven most boys become unable to walk. It is likely that by their late teens or twenties respiratory muscle weakness will make breathing harder; the heart may also be affected. Life expectancy will be shortened.

Becker Muscular Dystrophy

Becker muscular dystrophy is a milder form of dystrophy affecting males; Becker dystrophy progresses at a much slower rate. Symptoms may be noticed in childhood. These could include muscle cramps and poor performance in sports at school. Loss of mobility does not usually occur until adulthood.

Congenital myotonic dystrophy

Congenital myotonic dystrophy is present at birth; the baby is very weak and has difficulty sucking and swallowing. Motor development is delayed. There is usually some improvement in the early years; however there can be deterioration in late child hood and early adolescence. Some children with this type of dystrophy will start school using a wheelchair.

Myotonic dystrophy

Myotonic dystrophy sometimes becomes evident in late teens and early twenties although in a small number of cases symptoms can present during school years. It is characterised by a delayed relaxation of the muscles after contraction as well as muscle weakness. The muscles to be affected are the face, neck, hands, forearms and feet.

Spinal muscular atrophy (SMA)

There are several different types of SMA affecting children with differing onset ages and of differing severity. It can affect both boys and girls.

Type I (severe) – present at birth or shortly after birth. Children generally do not survive beyond the second year.

Type II (intermediate) – onset between 3 months and 2 years. The child is usually able to sit but not to stand unaided.

Type III (mild) – onset usually about 2 years. The child will be able to walk and will have a normal lifespan.

For further information contact:

Muscular Dystrophy Campaign
7–11 Prescott Place
London SW4 6BS

Tel: 020 7720 8055
www.muscular-dystrophy.org

The Jennifer Trust
for Spinal Muscular Atrophy
Elta House
Birmingham Road
Stratford-upon-Avon CV37 0AQ

Tel: 01789 267520
Helpline (Families only)
Tel: 0800 957 3100
www.jtsma.org.uk

Parent Project UK
PO Box 43178
London E17 3XA

Tel: 0208 281 4333
www.ppuk.org

Contact A Family
209–211 City Road
London EC1V 1JN

Tel: 020 7608 8700
www.cafamily.org.uk

Educational implications (muscular dystrophy)

It is important that pupils with the muscular dystrophy group of conditions are given experiences that add to their quality of life. Education provides opportunities for pupils with muscular dystrophy to have the same expectations and experiences as other pupils. It is important that pupils are prepared for adult life in the same way as their peers, regardless of the prognosis of their condition.

Planning for changing needs

Key stages have been used as a very general guide to the possible timescale for the progression of Duchenne muscular dystrophy. The prognosis for youngsters with Duchenne muscular dystrophy is now changing owing to the development of steroid treatment, which can in some cases extend mobility into the early teens, and ventilatory support, which can possibly increase life expectancy into their twenties.

Note: *Other dystrophy conditions may progress at a slower pace. Some pupils may start school using a wheelchair.*

Key stage 1

- Some pupils may start school before a diagnosis has been made.
- Parents may need a great deal of emotional support. This in turn can create a need for emotional support for staff who work closely with the pupil.
- Staff may request information about the condition and how it is likely to progress. Be aware that parents are unlikely to be able to pass on this type of general information. The Family Care Officer, who is employed by the Muscular Dystrophy Society and is based at the regional centre, could be contacted via the physiotherapist for staff INSET.
- Outside agencies gradually become involved. The physiotherapist is likely to be a regular visitor, providing training and monitoring of a physical management routine.
- Designation of space for a physical management routine should be implemented.
- Identification of special educational needs should flag up future needs for the statementing process with the LEA/educational psychologist/parents.

The following are difficulties which may be experienced by the pupil:

- If the pupil struggles to get up from the floor, encourage him/her to use the furniture to push up on. Discourage him from using the heads of other pupils for balancing when getting up from sitting in a group. Provide a chair as an alternative to sitting on the floor when transferring to standing from sitting becomes difficult. The physiotherapist and occupational therapist will monitor changes of position and advise on suitable seating.
- The pupil may have increasingly frequent falls in the playground, but adult oversight should be non-intrusive. The physiotherapist will advise on the level of adult intervention.

- Supervision when moving around the school is advisable. If support is unavailable, position the pupil near the teacher and adjust the pace of movement accordingly.

- Handrails may be required in the toilets next to urinals and in the cubicle to aid balance. They may also be needed next to external doors that have steps.

- If PE activities become demanding, provide activities that offer degrees of difficulty. Seek advice from the physiotherapist.

- Stamina levels can be affected, consider time tabling of strenuous activities such as PE or climbing the stairs to the ICT suite to the morning when the pupil is more likely to be fresh.

- Stamina can change as the week progresses. By Friday, the child may be falling more frequently but stamina may be improved after the weekend break. Fatigue related to late nights, could have a physical consequence.

- Physical performance can also be affected by minor ailments such as colds.

- Handwriting might become tiring. Introduce keyboard skills early so that the skill has been established before there is a need.

- Self-image can be affected. Some pupils become very passive and avoid making decisions. Staff should consider their own attitudes and approaches to ensure that the pupil with muscular dystrophy is allowed to be independent and to make his/her own decisions.

Key stage 2 (all of the above KS1 issues plus)

- A statement of Special Educational Needs is likely to be in place to provide additional adult support.

- The pupil may become progressively weaker and walking becomes restricted. A wheelchair is usually used by the end of key stage 2. A powered chair may boost the pupil's self-esteem.

- The physiotherapist is likely to introduce specialist equipment such as a standing frame and a wheelchair into the daily management routine. Standing frames can be timetabled for use in art and design and technology when other pupils are usually standing.

- Assistance will be needed when transferring between classroom chairs and wheelchairs. Support staff are required to attend a Moving and Handling training course.

- Oversight is generally required in the playground.

- Assistance is required to collect meals, possibly to cut up food. The occupational therapist may recommend lightweight cutlery.

- Access to a disabled toilet facility is required when the pupil is no longer able to use a standard toilet independently. Specialist equipment such as a hoist and commode chair may be required.

- Some pupils present challenging behaviour as their physical ability deteriorates.

Key stages 3 & 4 (all of the above KS1 & 2 issues plus)

- Most pupils with Duchenne muscular dystrophy are 'off their feet' by the time they begin secondary school. All moving and handling procedures will be carried out using a hoist and sling. This will be recommended at the appropriate time by the physiotherapist; a multi-disciplinary assessment is likely to be instigated to recommend moving and handling procedures.

- Mobility difficulties have implications for access to specialist teaching rooms in schools with several floors. Access to upper floors is possible with a stair climber to carry the pupil in a manual wheelchair.

- Hand skills become weaker; therefore, a lightweight word processor will be useful for recording written work. Keyboard skills should have been established in KS1 and 2.

- A compact keyboard may become necessary as the student's range of arm movement becomes limited.

- Stamina becomes a more significant issue. The support assistant may have to act as a scribe for longer pieces of work.

- Additional adult support is required for all physical tasks.

- The physical management programme becomes more complex as the condition progresses. Curriculum access is often compromised. A restricted curriculum may be necessary. Consult the Educational Psychologist.

- Students may be offered spinal surgery during their time in secondary school. This would have implications related to absence. Liaison with the relevant Hospital Tuition Service may be required.

- Careful planning for work experience placements is required.

- Post-16 provision planned with the expectation of future employment being a realistic goal.

Perthes disease

Definition

Perthes disease is a condition in which the head of the femur flattens due to temporary lack of a sufficient supply of blood to the area. Perthes disease is most common in boys between the ages of 4 and 10 and can run in families. It most commonly affects one hip although both hips can sometimes be affected.

Causes of Perthes

There is a flattening of the top of the femur, when the supply of blood to the area is insufficient, causing the surface of the bone to deteriorate. The following symptoms may occur when Perthes disease is suspected:

- limited mobility;
- hip movement impeded by stiffness;
- shortening of leg;
- constant pain in the thigh;
- problems with walking, often limping;
- painful knee;
- wasting of upper thigh muscles.

Treatment of Perthes

Treatment for this condition varies. Some children will attend regular hydrotherapy to help stop the hip from stiffening, to ease pain, help build up muscles and to hopefully regain the range of movement in their hips.

The prognosis is fairly good, especially if treatment is available in the early stages of the disease. Long-term deformity of the hip can be avoided if supplies of blood are encouraged into the affected area. This will ensure that fresh bone cells result within approximately one year. New bone will then re-form within the next few years.

This condition usually runs its course within two to four years.

For further information contact:

Contact A Family
209–211 City Road
London EC1V 1JW

Tel: 020 7608 8700
Helpline: 0808 808 355
www.caf.org.uk

The Perthes Association
15 Recreation Road
Guildford GU1 1HE

Tel: 01483 306637

email: admin@perthes.org.uk

Educational implications (Perthes disease)

Advice is usually available from the orthopaedic department or the physiotherapy department involved in the management of pupils with Perthes disease. Many pupils have residual pain and/or limited mobility, throughout the rehabilitation period.

The following are general considerations:

- Symptoms of joint pain and stiffness can vary from day to day.

- Rest is recommended for severe pain; some pupils require analgesia (pain killers) in school. Rest is best done at home if pain is severe.

- Restricted mobility may, in some cases, require use of a wheelchair over long distances. It is not usually necessary for pupils to stay in their wheelchairs within the classroom. This may have an impact on out-of-school visits and school transport arrangements.

- Pupils may have difficulty sitting on the floor during carpet time and assemblies.

- Prolonged sitting in examinations can contribute to discomfort. Additional rest breaks can be requested through the examinations officer.

- Low-impact exercise – walking, swimming, cycling – is very good for pupils with these conditions. High-impact sports and contact sports should be avoided.

- Pupils can generally be relied upon to be self-limiting in physical activities.

- Long absences from school are possible following orthopaedic surgery. In a minority of cases home tuition may be recommended.

- Close liaison between the family, health professionals and other relevant outside agencies will ensure changing needs can be met.

Prader-Willi Syndrome

Definition

The incidence is approximately 1:15,000 births and it occurs in both males and females. Pupils may exhibit any of the following characteristics:

- **hyperphagia** (excessive appetite) caused by a failure in the mechanism which tells a person that they have had sufficient food. Babies with PWS show little interest in feeding but between the ages of one and four interest in food increases and it can become an insatiable obsession. Some children can control food intake but others eat at every opportunity whether it be appropriate or not, e.g. taking other people's food, eating food from bins. Unless the diet is carefully controlled, weight gain can be very rapid and considerable problems result;

- **hypotonia** (low muscle tone) possibly resulting in speech problems, poor fine motor skills, poor gross motor skills and delayed toileting;

- **short stature** which results in height which is below average;

- **hypogonadism** causes delayed or arrested puberty;

- **temperature control** can be poor and there can be a risk of overheating or hypothermia;

- **high pain** threshold which can mask symptoms of illness and safety risks, e.g. danger from hot water;

- **eyesight problems** as a result of myopia (short-sightedness), strabismus (abnormal alignment of the two eyes) and nystagmus (involuntary movement of the eyes causing reduced depth perception, poor eye–hand co-ordination);

- **curvature of the spine** during the growing period;

- **dental or oral problems**; thick or sticky saliva resulting in 'crusting' at the corners of the mouth, a poor quality of tooth enamel and a small jaw resulting in overcrowding of the teeth;

- **speech and language delay**; expressive language is generally being more impaired than receptive language;

- **cognitive ability** varies from moderate to severe learning difficulty to a learning ability within the average range;

- **behavioural characteristics** which can include temper outbursts, resistance to change, obsessive and/or compulsive behaviour, possessiveness of items to which they are attached, stubbornness;

- **immature social skills** may be restricted and need to be taught; relationships with adults are usually good;

- **perseveration** can occur (i.e. persistent talking or questioning about a topic);
- **skin picking** can become obsessive and, owing to high pain thresholds, the pupil may not feel any discomfort; an increase in this activity can be related to stress;
- **friendly, sociable, kind and caring with a good sense of humour**.

Causes

PWS can be caused by more than one genetic abnormality; in 70% of cases the genetic abnormality is called a deletion, i.e. a piece of chromosome 15 inherited from the father is missing. In 20–30% of cases PWS occurs when 2 chromosome 15s are inherited from the mother and none from the father. It is thought that this results in a malfunction of the hypothalamus (an area of the brain), which is responsible for causing the symptoms of PWS.

Treatment

- hormone treatment to address growth issues;
- advice will be given from a wide range of health professionals, e.g. paediatricians, dieticians, physiotherapists, occupational therapists, speech and language therapists and professionals in education.

For further information contact:

The Prader-Willi Syndrome Association
125a London Road
Derby DE1 2QQ

Tel: 01332 365 676

www.pwsa-uk.demon.co.uk

Educational implications (Prader-Willi syndrome)

There are a number of issues which may need to be taken into consideration when supporting a pupil with Prader-Willi syndrome.

Diet

Diet has to be carefully monitored (calorie intake should be lower than that of other children), which has implications for portions given for school meals, food which is permissible at snack time and school parties. It may be helpful if the whole class group eats in a healthy manner in order to support their peer with PWS. Tuck shops, cafeteria-style catering and food technology lessons may also cause difficulties. Advice should be taken from parents. Supervision is needed as pupils may eat anything, whether it is suitable or not; stealing food is not unknown. Storage of lunchboxes should be away from the classroom.

Fine motor skills

Fine motor skills should be developed from the earliest stages. Alternative recording strategies and support to manipulate equipment may be required.

Gross motor skills

The younger pupil may require support to develop independent movement around school. Exercise is important: older pupils may need encouragement to take part in PE lessons and care should be taken when teams are being chosen so as not to leave the pupil with PWS until last.

Short stature

Consideration may need to be given in order to achieve access to equipment.

Delayed puberty

Sensitivity may be required when sex education lessons are given. Privacy may need to be given to teenage boys when changing for PE as physical development may be different from their peers.

Temperature regulation

Pupils with PWS may be either too hot or too cold and may need oversight and encouragement to wear the appropriate clothes for the weather.

Memory problems

The short-term memory required for remembering instructions may be limited, strategies to support this may be required. Consolidation and revision of skills and information learned will be necessary.

Poor vision related to Nystagmus, Strabismus and Myopia

Pupils may need longer to see objects, take longer to read print (which may necessitate longer time for examinations) and require larger print. They may need to be placed appropriately in the classroom to see the teacher and read information from the white board.

Daytime sleeping

Pupils may fall sleep during lessons. They should be encouraged to stay awake by moving to different activities of a short duration. If sleep is unavoidable help will be needed to catch up on information missed.

Delayed toilet training

Schools may need to implement a toilet training programme in conjunction with parents.

Behaviour problems

Routines are important: being aware of the signs of a temper tantrum and diffusing or distracting from the situation may help, together with a quiet area to calm down. Behaviour management strategies may be required.

Skin picking

An increase in this habit can be a sign of stress, so the pupil should be observed for causes. Praise should be given when skin is not picked.

Problems with saliva

The pupil should be encouraged to drink quantities of water.

High thresholds of pain

Be aware that the pupil with PWS has a high pain threshold. Check for injury after falls and monitor closely in potentially hazardous activities in lessons such as Design Technology.

Restricted growth (including achondroplasia)

Definition

Restricted growth may be the result of over one hundred medical conditions. They can be divided into two main categories, proportionate and disproportionate short stature.

Proportionate short stature (PSS)

Growth is restricted throughout the whole body and may be associated with chronic heart, lung, kidney or liver disease. In Turner's syndrome restricted growth may be the only symptom prior to puberty; however, learning difficulties are a common feature. Other growth disorders include Silver Russell syndrome, Soto's Syndrome, growth hormone insufficiency and premature sexual maturation.

Disproportionate short stature

Many conditions and diseases can cause disproportionate short stature, which is a relatively normal torso with short limbs and possibly a skull which may be different in appearance. Some conditions have a primary bone disorder called skeletal dysplasia, achondroplasia being the most common. Hypochondroplasia is a similar condition but the abnormalities are less apparent.

Achondroplasia

During foetal and early development, cartilage develops into bone. For those children with achondroplasia, the rate of this change is disturbed, resulting in short bones and reduced height. It occurs in about 1 in 20,000 births, affecting males and females in equal proportions.

Pupils with achondroplasia may exhibit the following characteristics:

- relatively normal torso and short arms and legs;
- large skull;
- straight upper back with a markedly curved lower spine;
- loose joints;
- lower legs can become bowed;
- low back and leg pains;

- normal intelligence;
- over-crowded teeth;
- reduced muscle tone;
- increased weight;
- frequent middle ear infections causing some hearing loss;
- breathing difficulties caused by a small chest, large tonsils and a small facial structure.

Causes

The main cause of PSS is considered to be a lack of growth hormones produced by the thyroid and pituitary glands. Chromosomal defects in girls with Turner's syndrome can result in changes in growth rates.

Achondroplasia is a genetic disorder of bone growth. It is caused by an abnormal gene on one of the chromosome '4 pair'.

Treatment

There is no specific treatment which can reverse the effects of restricted growth conditions. Hormone treatment can be used in some cases to improve growth rates. Pupils may receive input from a variety of health professionals, e.g. dieticians, physiotherapists, occupational therapists. Surgical options may also be considered including limb lengthening.

For further information contact:

Bone Dysplasia Group
C/o Child Growth Foundation
2 Mayfield Avenue
Chiswick
London W4 1PW

Tel: 020 8994 7625
Fax: 020 8995 9075

Restricted Growth Association
PO Box 8919
Birmingham B27 6DQ

Tel: 01308 898445
E-mail rga1@talk21.com
www.rgaonline.org.uk

Child Growth Foundation
2 Mayfield Ave
Chiswick
London W4 1PW

Tel: 020 8994 7625
Fax: 020 8995 9075

Dwarf Athletic Association UK
PO Box 76
Stockport
Cheshire SK4 5JJ

Tel: 0161 431 6156

Educational implications (restricted growth)

Not all pupils with restricted growth will have learning difficulties. Some pupils will be late in reaching developmental milestones, but ultimately overall development is usually normal.

Pupils with short stature may experience difficulties related to self-esteem, inappropriate peer expectations and physical access. The following are points which should be considered:

- Expectations: be aware that both adults and their peers should treat these pupils appropriately. Monitor playground behaviour.

- If limb-lengthening surgery is planned, please refer to the advice contained within club foot (Talipes).

- Seating: consider height of chairs and desks.

- Position in the classroom: give consideration not only to a pupil's size, but also to possible sensory defects, such as hearing loss or visual impairment.

- Movement between lessons: carrying equipment and bags.

- Access to equipment and materials in practical lessons: consider positioning of equipment on the table in the room.

- Fine motor skills: pupils with short, stubby fingers may need adapted fine motor equipment, such as pencils and scissors. The aim should be to facilitate independent access to the school curriculum, using the minimum of adaptations and additional support.

- PE lessons: check with parents whether there are any restrictions on physical activities. Generally, contact sports and other high impact activities, such as jumping, are not advisable. Pupils with achondroplasia, should avoid gymnastics and contact sports because of the potential for neck or back damage, due to existing spinal stenosis (narrow spinal canal, particularly in the lower back). PE staff should be made aware of any contra-indications. The Dwarf Athletic Association UK can give advice on teaching sporting skills in school.

- Independence skills: making minor adaptations to the school and classroom environment can easily foster independence. For example provision of:
  - a lower coat hook in the cloakroom;
  - a lower handrail on staircases;
  - a step near the toilet and wash hand basins, extended tap turners;
  - lower door handles, light switches, locks on toilet doors;
  - use of glass in lower sections of doors, to ensure visibility;
  - dressing aids, as prescribed by OT.

Spina bifida

Definitions

Spina bifida is a fault in the spinal column in which one or more vertebrae fail to form properly. This leaves a gap or split, which causes damage to the central nervous system.

1. Spina bifida occulta (hidden)

- the outer part of the vertebrae are not completely formed;
- a very mild common form: in the majority of cases it is of no consequence at all;
- one in ten of the population may have this condition;
- in rare cases, the spinal cord becomes trapped causing functioning problems.

2. Spina bifida cystica (cyst like)

a) Meningocele: This is the least common form; a sac containing tissues covers the spinal cord and cerebro fluid. The fluid protects the cord and brain. Damage rarely occurs.

b) Myelomeningocele: This is the most serious and more common form. The cyst not only contains tissues and cerebro-spinal fluid but also nerves and part of the spinal cord. The cord is damaged or not properly developed. This always results in paralysis and loss of sensation below the damaged region.

3. Cranium bifida

The bones of the skull fail to form properly. The sac that forms is known as encephalocele. It may contain only cerebro-spinal fluid. It can contain part of the brain, resulting in brain damage.

Cause

There is no known reason why spina bifida occurs.

Treatment

Lesions in the spine are either repaired shortly after birth or left to close on their own.

For further information contact:

Association for Spina Bifida and Hydrocephalus (ASBAH)
42 Park Road
Peterborough PE1 2UQ

Tel: 01733 555988
www.asbah.org

Educational implications (spina bifida)

- Pupils with spina bifida will vary in both their physical and cognitive ability according to the type of damage caused by their condition.

- Many pupils with diagnosed cases of spina bifida occulta and meningocele spina bifida will be ambulant but may be late in reaching developmental milestones. Bladder and bowel control can be late; in some cases it is never achieved. Catheterisation and bowel management may be required.

- Pupils who have myelomeningocele spina bifida are likely to be wheelchair users although therapeutic walking and standing with a walking or standing frame may be introduced into the physical management routine. Bowel and bladder incontinence are likely to be present.

- Many pupils with spina bifida also have hydrocephalus and will have a shunt in their brain to drain excess cerebral fluid. Hydrocephalus can result in a range of learning difficulties. Refer to page 44 for guidance.

An inter-disciplinary assessment will inform school of the individual needs of the pupil. The following are general points to consider:

- awareness raising of any medical needs through an individual health care plan;

- plan movement times to take account of restricted mobility necessitating use of a wheelchair or mobility aids;

- consider access issues relating to difficulty climbing stairs or accessing the first floor in a wheelchair;

- the pupil may have difficulty sitting on the floor during carpet time and assembly;

- PE lessons may require differentiation;

- a physical management routine may need to be incorporated in the school day – by whom, when and where will it be implemented?

- plan for liaison time with outside agencies;

- budget for funding to release staff for training in the use of specialised equipment;

- if manipulation of standard classroom equipment is difficult, is specialised equipment or a compensatory approach required?

- reorganise positioning of equipment to aid independent access;

- support the pupil in the organisation of his/her personal effects such as the school bag;

- facilitate disabled toilet access with appropriate moving and handling equipment;

- plan for support assistants to assist with personal care issues taking planned and unplanned staff absences into consideration;

- plan carefully for out of school visits;

- include careful planning for work experience placements;

- home/school transport may be required.

Health care considerations for pupils with spina bifida

Pupils with spina bifida frequently have a loss of sensation below the site of their lesion and as a consequence do not feel pain.

Care should be taken when:

- assisting the pupil with transfers between wheelchairs and classroom chairs;

- supporting the pupil in assisted physical activities such as walking with a rollator;

- applying and removing orthoses;

- positioning the pupil near heat sources (radiators, water pipes, sunshine);

- using potentially hazardous substances in science and D&T.

Support staff may be asked to monitor skin condition and pressure point areas for signs of skin change.

Some pupils with spina bifida may be bowel and/or bladder incontinent and will require support for personal hygiene issues. This may include catheterisation.

Pupils who have hydrocephalus and have a shunt fitted will require additional health care strategies. Refer to page 44.

Spinal injuries

Definition

An injury to the spinal cord is a very severe blow to the body's central nervous system which results in the body going into 'shock'. This can last from a few hours to several weeks. It can result in paralysis, an inability to move or feel parts of the body. The higher the point of injury in the spine, the greater the extent of functional loss.

Tetraplegia (or quadriplegia)

Tetraplegia is a high level injury which occurs as a result of a broken neck or injury to the spine in the neck area. It causes part or full paralysis in all four limbs and affects the chest muscles which can cause breathing difficulties.

Paraplegia

This is a low level injury which occurs as a result of damage to the middle and lower back and causes paralysis to the legs and abdomen. The amount of remaining movement in the trunk and chest depends on the point of injury.

Autonomic paralysis

The autonomic nervous system controls the involuntary functions of the internal organs and glands and is connected to the spinal cord. Spinal injuries cause damage to this system, affecting the function of the bowel, bladder and the circulation of the blood. In some cases, the spinal cord is only partly damaged which allows some messages to pass from the brain to the muscles and organs of the body. This allows some people to have some movements in their legs. There are a number of different types of incomplete spinal cord injuries resulting in varied loss of sensation and movement and allowing some degree of recovery.

Causes

An injury to the spinal cord can be caused by accidental injuries, viral infection, cysts or tumours on or near to the spinal cord.

Treatment

- hospitalisation for a long period following the trauma;
- assessments by specialist services to provide equipment;
- catheterisation to drain urine; sometimes surgery to by pass bladder/bowel;
- physical management by physiotherapist and occupational therapist to achieve maximum functional independence.

For further information contact:

Spinal Injuries Association, 76 St James Lane, London N10 3DF

Tel: 0800 980 0501 (Free phone helpline) www.spinal.co.uk
email: sia@spinal.co.uk

Low level injuries occurring below the waist are likely to result in the following physical difficulties:

- loss of mobility;
- bowel and bladder incontinence;
- susceptibility to pressure sores;
- reduced stamina.

High level injuries occurring in the neck area are likely to result in the following physical difficulties:

- loss of mobility;
- bowel and bladder incontinence;
- susceptibility to pressure sores;
- susceptibility to autonomic shock syndrome (see below)
- reduced stamina;
    AND
- loss or restriction in fine motor skills affecting:
    - self help skills, e.g. eating/drinking/dressing/grooming;
    - recording skills.

It is unlikely that the cognitive ability of pupils who have sustained a spinal injury will be altered after the accident. Their learning will be significantly affected by reduced stamina and possibly problems relating to self esteem.

Refer to later sections on the following areas for possible strategies to deal with:

- accessing the building,
- mobility issues;
- planning out-of-school visits;
- accessing the curriculum;
- alternative recording strategies;
- dealing with emotional issues;
- writing an individual health care plan (IHCP);
- joint protection issues, which will require further advice from the occupational and physiotherapists.

Autonomic dysreflexia

This is an emergency condition requiring immediate attention. The individual health care plan should be very detailed and concise.

Autonomic dysreflexia is an abnormal response to a problem such as an over-full bowel or bladder; it can also happen as a result of pressure sores, broken skin, burns and ingrown toenails.

Symptoms can include:

- Pounding headache (caused by raised blood pressure);
- goose pimples;
- sweating above the level of injury;
- nasal congestion;
- slow pulse;
- blotching of the skin;
- restlessness;
- flushed (reddened) face;
- nausea;
- cold, clammy skin below level of spinal injury.

Action to take:

1. Send someone to contact parents or carers.
2. If symptoms are giving cause for concern ring for an ambulance before contacting the parents.
3. Keep the pupil in an upright position.
4. Try to identify the cause of the problem and deal with it if practical, e.g.
   - catheterise to relieve bladder pressure;
   - loosen clothing to reveal pressure sore or toenail problem;
   - remove any orthoses to check skin condition.
5. Observe closely to see if symptoms improve.
6. Pass accurate information to the paramedics.
7. Update parents/carers as soon as possible.

Rare conditions

- A 'rare' condition is defined as one that affects less than 1 in 20,000.

- There are presently more than 6,000 known rare disorders and the number is increasing all the time due to medical advancements. They are usually genetically linked, or the result of a viral infection.

- Once a group of symptoms has been identified in a number of individuals, it is given a name that is either descriptive of the condition or named after the medical specialist/s involved in the initial identification.

- The majority are classed as 'syndromes', or 'diseases'.

- Some conditions are evident from birth, while others develop over a period of time.

- If you are informed that a pupil in your class may have a suspected condition, record any academic, physical, or emotional difficulties that you have noticed.

- Keep accurate records, since these are particularly useful to the medical profession in helping to identify a condition.

- The teacher's approach should always be to look at the difficulties the pupil is experiencing and remediate, following the guidelines in the new Code of Practice.

- If there is no improvement the class teacher should involve the SENCO, who would make a decision whether to refer the pupil to the educational psychologist, the school nurse and SCMO, or sensory support staff, depending on need.

- Sudden changes, or deterioration of abilities, should be reported back to the family and any support staff involved immediately.

- Once a diagnosis is made, treatment, if appropriate, would begin. This may include regular medication and the identification of 'warning signs' that require immediate medical attention. In most cases an IHCP will need to be written.

- Information about individual conditions can be found in the 'Contact a Family' (CaF) Directory or from internet sites.

Useful websites:	
Nord (National Organisation of Rare Disorders)	www.rarediseases.org
Office of Rare Diseases	http://rarediseases.info.nih.gov/
Rare Genetic Diseases in Children	http://mcrcr2.med.nyu.edu/murphp01/homenew.htm
Canadian Organisation for Rare Disorders	www.cord.ca/

Section 2

Meeting the pupil's physical needs

Meeting the educational implications of the individual pupil's physical needs – whose responsibility?

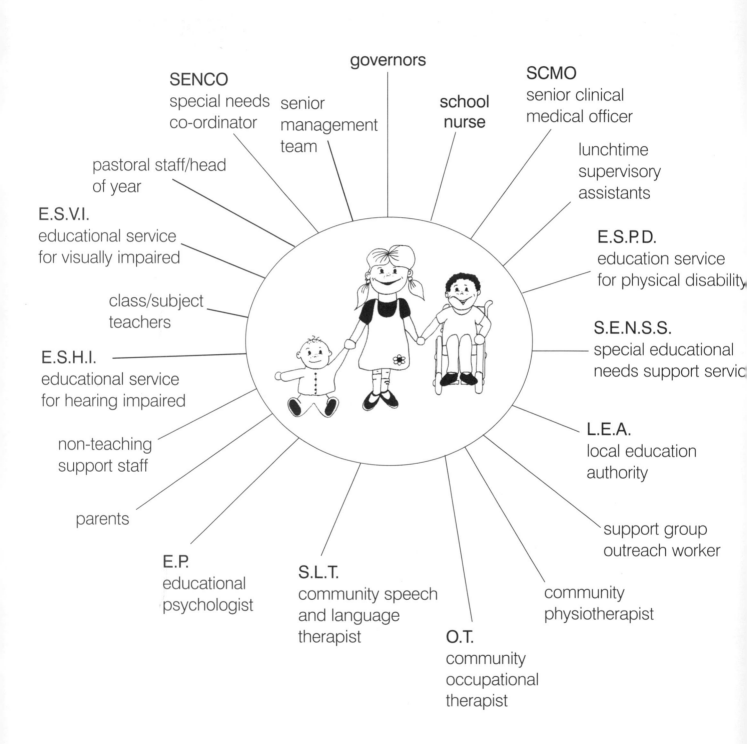

governors

SENCO
special needs
co-ordinator

senior
management
team

school
nurse

SCMO
senior clinical
medical officer

pastoral staff/head
of year

lunchtime
supervisory
assistants

E.S.V.I.
educational service
for visually impaired

E.S.P.D.
education service
for physical disability

class/subject
teachers

S.E.N.S.S.
special educational
needs support service

E.S.H.I.
educational service
for hearing impaired

L.E.A.
local education
authority

non-teaching
support staff

support group
outreach worker

parents

E.P.
educational
psychologist

S.L.T.
community speech
and language
therapist

O.T.
community
occupational
therapist

community
physiotherapist

Individual Health Care Plan

Not all pupils with medical needs will require an individual health care plan (IHCP).

An individual health care plan is intended to summarise a pupil's medical needs, identify what is an emergency for that pupil and agree a procedure to be followed.

It should ensure that school staff have sufficient information to understand and support a pupil with long-term medical needs.

The school should write the IHCP, in consultation with the parents and a health care professional. This could be the school nurse or a hospital based liaison nurse. In some cases it is difficult to meet with all representatives together.

It is acceptable to write a draft IHCP and circulate it to all interested parties for comments.

The IHCP should be amended when necessary and reviewed annually. Additional documentation is required for consent to administer medication in schools.

See Supporting Pupils with Medical Needs DH&E Circular 14/98 for further information.

Appendix 2 – Individual Health Care Plan

Risk assessments

It is the school's responsibility to carry out risk assessments. Risk assessments are required when a potential hazard has been identified and measures are needed to reduce the risk of that hazard occurring.

Increasingly, health professionals are required to carry out risk assessments relating to moving and handling pupils. These can be used to inform an individual risk assessment within school.

When preparing a risk assessment related to supporting an individual pupil, it is acceptable to cross reference the risk assessment and individual health care plan, to avoid duplication of work.

It is important that all staff, who regularly move and handle pupils who have physical difficulties, attend an appropriate Moving and Handling training course.

Access to buildings

Recent Legislation

The 'SEN and Disability Rights in Education' Bill (2001) recommends that schools carefully consider their planning for pupils with special needs.

It states that there is a clear responsibility for schools to *anticipate* the needs of pupils with special educational needs. The main points from the Bill are listed below.

- LEAs and schools have a *joint* responsibility to meet the needs of pupils with special needs.

- These needs must be taken into consideration and planned for well in advance, e.g. time-tabling pupils for the ground floor, if there are safety issues with stairs.

- To ensure *equality of provision*, schools should provide *equivalent provision* on the ground floor if necessary, e.g. if subject provision or the SEN base is on the first floor or above.

- If buildings are being modified or a new-build is planned, the special needs of pupils must be borne in mind.

- It is anticipated that schools write an 'Access Plan' to ensure access for all pupils. This should be in place by April 2003.

Accessing the building for pupils with mild physical disabilities, e.g. hemiplegia, short stature

The head teacher and school governors will need to undertake a site inspection with either the site access officer or health and safety representative and consider the issues listed below.

- Do all external and internal steps have grab bars for the pupils use?

- Do all flights of stairs have handrails on both sides for safety?

- Are there any sunken mat wells that could be a trip hazard?

- Are all steps easily visible with a contrast between tread and wall?

- Can the pupil open all doors independently?

- Is the accessible toilet facility clearly marked and free of clutter?

- Is there an area, e.g. medical room, that can be used for a physical management programme?

Accessing the building for wheelchair-users

These additional questions relate to wheelchair-users.

- Does each subject area/building have at least one level entry door?
- If there are ramps already in situ, do they comply with the latest guidelines regarding angle of slope? Are they fitted with either a concrete lip and/or handrails to ensure safety?
- Are corridors free of clutter?
- Are all doors wide enough for wheelchair-users to get through?
- Is there clear access *into* all classrooms, e.g. no cupboards next to/behind doors restricting space?
- Do fire doors in corridors open easily?
  - If not, encourage pupils to ask the nearest person to open the door for them – this aids social skills.
  - Newly built schools/blocks are having electro-magnetic door-stops fitted which are linked to Fire Alarm system.
- Are there short flights of internal stairs? Can they be ramped?
- How will upper floors be accessed? Is there a lift large enough to be used by wheelchair users?
  - If not, the use of a stair climber may need to be considered.

(a) Stair Climber in use   **(b) Stair Climber**[1]

- What procedure will staff follow in case of a fire when a pupil is above the ground floor?
  - If in doubt consult your local Fire Safety Officer.

Areas of concern, which are not easily remedied, should be noted by the headteacher or site access officer, who will then need to contact the SEN office for advice.

---

1 By kind permission of Advanced Stair Lifts UK

Mobility issues

The following are issues that need to be considered for pupils who are independently mobile, but have some problems, e.g. hemiplegia, short stature:

- Always ensure that mobility aids, such as sticks and rollators (walking frames on wheels), are to hand and not a trip hazard to other pupils.

- The pupil may need to leave class a few minutes early to avoid crowded corridors and stairs.

- If the pupil requires adult oversight for movement between classes, try to provide distance supervision. This allows the pupil to maintain and develop friendships and independence.

- If the pupil needs closer supervision on the stairs, ensure the support assistant walks *beside* the pupil not *behind*.

- It may be appropriate to give verbal prompts to hold the handrail and/or move one step at a time for safety.

- The identification of 'drop off' points or provision of a locker would reduce the amount of equipment/books carried by the pupil at any one time.

When planning an outing arrange a pre-visit to check the site, stairs, distances to walk.

Additionally, for pupils in wheelchairs,

ensure support staff know the most easily accessible route to all subject areas:

- Look at classroom layout – is there sufficient room to negotiate around the classroom or at least get to areas that the pupil needs to access?

- If appropriate, ensure support staff know the location of the lift/storage place for the stair climber and how often to charge it.

- Ensure that a sufficient number of staff are trained to use the stair climber to cover absences and that retraining is arranged at 6–12 month intervals to cover safety regulations.

- Ensure all staff are aware of the fire drill for that particular pupil, where the nearest fire exit is, and whether it is wheelchair-friendly.

- When planning an outing, again, arrange a pre-visit to check the site and whether all areas are accessible to wheelchairs. If not, find out if there are alternative activities available.

Adapted furniture

The aim of using adapted furniture is twofold:

i) to provide and maintain a good working position;

For example, the pupil should always sit on a chair with feet flat on the floor, with bottom well back in the seat, back straight and head in the midline to ensure a stable base (see 'Classroom organisation').

A pupil who constantly leans to one side could possibly develop a curvature of the spine. Additionally visual perception might be affected by distortion.

ii) to ensure physical safety.

- A pupil with poor balance may require a chair with sides as well as a back.
- At Nursery/Infant level a small Captain's chair (seat height 28 cm) may be appropriate.
- To stop the pupil slipping forward in the chair put a non-slip mat on the seat.

- At senior level in subjects such as science, D&T, where the pupil would normally sit on a stool, either a science chair (right) or for more security an adjustable height 'perching stool' (left) covers the safety aspect.
- The pupil may also require an angled cushion to improve sitting posture and/or a foot block to ensure that feet are flat.

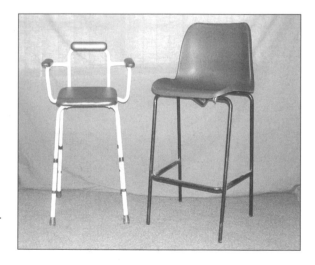

There are a number of commercially available foot blocks. These range from moulded plastic, which are generally used to aid toileting, to wooden stacking foot blocks which provide a choice of heights.

If the pupil's physical requirements are greater than those mentioned here, a full seating assessment by a paediatric occupational therapist should be requested.

Some pupils will require a different height of table at which to work.

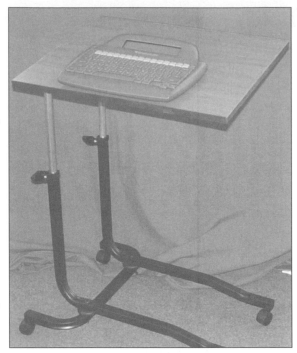

- The simplest solution is to provide 'leg raisers' (to increase height), or some schools are happy to reduce the height of one of the tables already in a particular subject area, if a smaller table is required.

- Small mobile, adjustable-angled cantilever tables (see right) are fairly cheap, readily available and adequate for most situations. This would, for example, go over a wheelchair in any classroom environment.

- More substantial tables such as the Vari-tech 'Vari-table' would be more appropriate, e.g. in art, at secondary level.

- Additionally, there is a wide range of height-adjustable tables now available for both the secondary and primary setting. These may be used as standard classroom furniture for individual or groups of pupils.

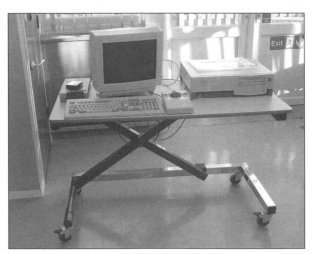

- When planning for inclusion, secondary schools might also look at the range of specialised variable-height tables, available for use in ICT (see left), D&T, food technology. (See section on supporting D&T).

- For a pupil with a condition requiring careful positioning for posture and possible neck problems, the use of a copy-book holder, or adjustable angle board for reading, are beneficial.

Toilet adaptations

Most schools now have a standard accessible toilet facility, but this may not meet the needs of all pupils. Different medical conditions have different toileting requirements which will need to be met within this facility. It should also be available for use by disabled staff and visitors.

Certain factors should be taken into consideration when planning to meet the needs of pupils with toileting difficulties.

Location

- Is the accessible toilet facility centrally sited?
- Is it available for the use of both sexes and well-signed?
- Is the entrance free of clutter?
- Is it well-lit, does it have independent heating and is it in good decorative order?
- Is the emergency light easily visible to passing staff?

Initial considerations

Even standard equipment may need to be adapted to suit individual needs, e.g.

- lever taps are more appropriate for pupils with limited physical ability;
- an electric hand dryer is easier to use than a paper towel dispenser;
- the toilet roll/paper holder could be sited on one of the drop-down bars for easy access;
- a toilet seat insert and foot block may be necessary for younger pupils;
- if the pupil is able to use the same toilet facilities as the rest of the class, grab bars may be required for safety – N.B. mark the height with the pupil present to ensure the bars are in the correct position.

Range of use

Is the accessible toilet facility large enough to support the full range of medical needs?

Does it have a sufficient area available for nappy changing purposes?

- Nursery-aged pupils should be changed standing up, if they have standing balance. This protects support staff from developing back problems.
- For pupils who are unable to stand, a table (plinth) is more appropriate. N.B. A height-adjustable plinth is better for staff to work at, than the static kind.

Are there wash-down facilities or space for these to be installed?

- A level entry shower is the best option, since this gives maximum potential usage.
- Shower controls should be height adjustable and the temperature regulated for safety and to encourage development of independent washing skills.

What are the disposal requirements?

- Products with normal body waste, e.g. nappies, can be double black-bagged and put into the usual school bins.
- Used catheters and colostomy bags need to be placed in yellow bags and an arrangement set up for disposal – either send them home with the pupil for parents to dispose of, or contact the local council who will arrange a collection.

Are there storage facilities for medical supplies?

- Are the upper cupboards the correct height for easy reach and safety?
- Is there a flat surface available on which to set out resources needed for semi-sterile procedures, e.g. changing a colostomy bag?

Additional requirements for pupils in electric-powered wheelchairs

- Is there room within the facility for the pupil to manoeuvre his/her electric-powered wheelchair?
- Is the door wide enough for easy access? Does the door open outwards giving maximum area for movement within the toilet?

Pupils might also need:

- a commode, or moulded toilet chair, which should be assessed and prescribed by the paediatric occupational therapist;
- either a mobile, or ceiling track hoist, used with a sling, for transfers between chair and toilet/commode – this would normally be initiated by the paediatric physiotherapist/occupational therapist, who would advise and liaise as necessary with the company;
- the school would need to arrange equipment checks based on the recommendations of the suppliers after the first year's warranty is finished to ensure safety;
- staff would also need to be trained in ergonomic moving and handling to ensure that correct procedures are carried out – this would usually be arranged through the LEA.

Intimate care procedures

"Intimate care is care which involves contact with parts of the body that we usually consider to be private." Barnardo's Carers' Handbook.

The term 'intimate care procedures' can include toileting and cleansing routines, catheterisation, urostomy care, colostomy care and emergency administration of rectal medication.

Specific training for catheterisation, urostomy and colostomy care and emergency administration of rectal medication must be provided by a health care professional before schools implement these routines.

Care routines should be documented in an individual health care plan (IHCP).

The legal framework

1. Duties and responsibilities

Members of staff often have concerns regarding their obligation to administer medicines in school. 'Supporting Pupils With Medical Needs In School', Circular 14/96, DfEE gives the following advice:

"Employers (usually the LEA or governing body) should ensure that their insurance policies provide appropriate cover for staff willing to support pupils with medical needs. ... Subject to this point, there is no legal or contractual duty on staff to administer medicine or supervise a pupil taking it. This is a voluntary role. Support staff may have specific duties to provide medical assistance as part of their contract." para. 13

"Teachers and other school staff have a common law duty to act as any reasonably prudent parent would to make sure pupils are healthy and safe on school premises and this might in exceptional circumstances extend to administering medicine and/or taking action in an emergency." para. 14
DfEE circular 14/96 'Supporting Pupils with Medical Needs in Schools.'

It is important that the support assistant's job description specifies support for personal hygiene routines and administration of medication.

2. Accommodation

The *Education (School Premises) Regulations 1996* requires schools to provide accommodation to give medical and dental treatment and care for pupils during school hours (this may not be its sole use).

Also they must ensure:

- safe storage and handling of medicines (this could also include medical supplies, e.g. catheters);
- that medication required in emergency situations, is not locked away;
- relevant staff know the location of medicines.

3. Staffing

Staff must

- be willing to carry out the procedure;
- have the role included in their job description;
- receive formal training and be assessed as competent by a named professional, to whom they can refer to advice and further training.

Where possible, two adults, one of the same gender, should be present for intimate or invasive procedures, to minimise the potential for allegations of abuse. (This is not essential or necessarily desirable for toilet training and self-management routines.)

The Chailey Heritage Guidelines for Good Practice in Intimate Care make a number of suggestions.

1. Every pupil should be treated with dignity and respect.
2. The pupil's right to privacy should be ensured, taking into consideration their age and the situation.
3. The pupil should be involved, wherever possible, in their own intimate care routines: explain what you are doing and ask, for their compliance.
4. Staff should be responsive to a pupil's reactions. If the pupil appears to be distressed or uncomfortable, stop and try another approach.
5. Make sure that practice in intimate care is as consistent as possible. Agree approaches with other care staff and document agreed procedures in the IHCP.
6. Never attempt to carry out a procedure for which you have not been trained. It is the school's responsibility to ensure that sufficient numbers of staff have been trained to cover for unexpected staff absences.
7. If you have any concerns about your duties or the pupil's reaction to your work, report it – the SENCO will advise on how to proceed.
8. Encourage pupils to have a positive image of their own body – never show distaste at any of the intimate care procedures that have to be carried out for the pupil.

Introducing toilet training

Incontinence can be a part of a medical condition or can be part of a global delay. Some children will never be totally continent so the emphasis will be on management of the condition. Other children will be late in achieving developmental milestones and toilet training will be delayed accordingly.

A child will pass through three stages as they develop bladder control:

1. The child becomes aware of having a wet or dirty nappy.
2. He/she knows urination is taking place and may indicate this.
3. The child realises he/she needs to urinate and may say so in advance.

Toilet training will be more successful if the child is at the last stage.

Assess the child over a period of two weeks to determine:

- if there is a pattern to when the child is wet or dirty;
- the indicators the child is giving that he/she needs the toilet (actions, facial expression);
- hourly visits to the toilet and monitoring of wet, soiled or dirty nappies should help to determine toileting behaviour and show an emerging pattern.

Some strategies to support the process:

- familiarise the child with the toilets, use other children as good models (being sensitive to their privacy), flush the toilets, wash hands etc.;
- encourage the child to use the toilet when he/she is indicating in some way that there is a need, but do not force the issue;
- take the child to the toilet at a time that the monitoring had indicated the child usually opens his bowels;
- ensure the child is able to reach and is comfortable on the toilet;
- stay with the child, talk to him/her, or take a book/toy to make the experience more relaxed;
- the child may not always use the toilet;
- it may take time to develop the idea of what is expected; don't become anxious;
- praise the child when the toilet is used;
- there may be some setbacks (possibly an emotional reason), patiently continue;
- accidents will occur – deal with them discreetly and without fuss;
- it may take time – be patient and success will be very satisfying.

It is important to develop a common home/school approach in order for the process to succeed.

Bowel incontinence

Some pupils with specific medical conditions may never achieve complete bowel continence. The parents or carers usually carry out most of the bowel management at home. This may include regular enemas and use of laxatives. Both parents and pupils need to be confident that any soiling issues can be dealt with discreetly in school whilst the youngster is working towards independent management of his/her condition. It is important that a common approach is used at home and at school with agreed strategies and rewards. It should be acknowledged that this can be a long process with setbacks along the way.

Consider the following points:

- sensitive sharing of information regarding the condition with relevant staff;

- access to a private toilet facility with waste disposal and washing facilities, note – some pupils prefer not to use the 'disabled toilet' facility;

- arrangements to enable the pupil to leave the classroom discreetly, when necessary;

- arrangements to ensure a supply of clean underwear and wet wipes;

- access to drinks, as a regular fluid-intake is usually recommended;

- consider toilet arrangements for school outings – a RADAR key gives access to all public disabled toilet facilities. (Parents can contact their local council to buy a key for a nominal sum.)

Self-management in early years

- Emphasis should be placed on establishing a routine where the pupil checks his/her nappy/trainer pants/underwear, for signs of soiling at regular intervals. Initially, this should be on arrival, at playtime, before going home (for part-time placements), lunchtimes and playtime.

- The supporting adult should use a low-key approach, acknowledging when the pupil identifies correctly that he/she needs changing, but never showing disappointment that the nappy is soiled. Remember this is a medical condition and may not be in the pupil's control.

- Always encourage the pupil to get his/her own things ready. A pictorial cue card helps to establish this routine.

- Additional visits to the toilet will be required to deal with soiling incidents, identified by smell.

- Nappies can be disposed of by double wrapping in plastic bags and placing in a bin, which is emptied by the caretaker in the usual way.

- Alternatively, a clinical waste collection service can be set up with the local council, who will arrange for a "yellow bag" collection.

Self-management in key stage 1

- Building on the work done in Early Years, the pupil will be encouraged to initiate visits to the toilet at regular intervals.

- Consider use of a token system – the pupil places a token on the teacher's desk as he/she leaves the room to go to the toilet and collects it on return.

- The support assistant is not required to be in the classroom at all times. A system should be established whereby support staff can be summoned when necessary. Some schools use walkie-talkies to keep in touch and others use staff timetables to locate support staff.

- The pupil should be encouraged to take responsibility for as much of the cleansing and changing routine as is possible.

- Adapt the pictorial cue card to suit the pupil's reading ability/cognitive development.

- Gradually withdraw 'hands-on' support.

- Monitoring of progress by a member of the senior management team can be a good motivator.

Self-management in key stage 2

- Pupils should now be encouraged to implement their cleansing and changing routines independently, with oversight for emotional support and guidance. Some pupils respond well to using an alarm on their wrist-watch, to alert them to the time to go to the toilet.

- It is hoped that independence will have been achieved well before secondary school transfer. Peer pressure plays an important role with older pupils, who become anxious if anybody knows about their condition.

Self-management in key stages 3 & 4

- Pupils generally manage their own cleansing and changing routines at KS3 & 4.

- Pupils should be given their own key to the designated toilet, if it is usually kept locked.

- It is essential that staff are sensitive to a pupil's need for privacy.

- SENCOs should ensure that a system is in place to inform temporary staff of any established routines, especially if a pupil needs to leave the room during lessons.

- Some pupils may experience emotional problems around puberty and can begin to deny that they have a problem. In a few cases counselling by a clinical psychologist may be necessary. Referrals can be made via the senior clinical medical officer (School Doctor).

My changing routine
Name:...

Step 1: get clean pants ready

Step 2: use the wipes to clean up

Step 3: wrap everything in a plastic bag

Step 4: put the bag in the bin

WASH HANDS

Step 5: wash hands

Section 3

Access to the curriculum

Classroom organisation

Arrangement of furniture

- Can wheelchair users enter the classroom without having to move furniture? Try to leave a clear access route to the pupil's desk.

- Is there a clear route for pupils with crutches or other walking aids to reach their desk? Encourage all pupils to keep the aisles clear of obstacles.

Sitting position – good practice

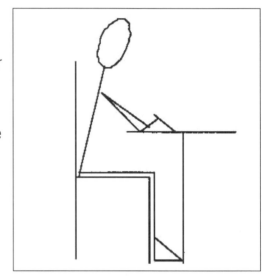

- Does the pupil have a good posture when sitting? Try to encourage a whole class approach to monitoring sitting position. Aim for feet flat on the floor, bottom to the back of the chair, back straight, head in the middle.

- Place left handers next to each other to reduce arm conflict.

- Provision of a sloping writing surface can improve the working position and consequently the quality of handwriting. Consider the use of a commercial sloping board or an empty arch lever file.

Position of pupil in relation to teacher/board

- Does the pupil have any sensory impairment? If so, try to ensure they sit facing the teacher/board wherever possible.

- Place pupils with poor copying skills in the middle of the classroom – reducing the angle of eye-to-board-to-book movements. Avoid placing them at the back as they will have too many interfering movements between them and the board.

Copying from the board

- Does the pupil have difficulty copying from the board? Try using different coloured chalks/pens for each line, or writing key words in different colours, or quarter the board so that the pupil knows which quarter is being copied from.

General classroom resources/specialist resources

- Can the pupil reach equipment from his/her chair or when seated in his/her wheelchair? Provide an individual set of equipment for pupils with limited mobility or restricted growth, so that they do not have to rely on help from others.

Deployment of support staff

- Use a colour-highlighted register to help identify pupils with specific needs, e.g. green = pupil with recording difficulties, blue = consider position in class (helps new and temporary teachers).

- IEPs should list areas of weaknesses (and strengths), e.g. list of key weaknesses down one side of IEP with relevant weaknesses circled and strengths underlined.

- The primary role of the support assistant is to facilitate independent learning. However, there are two main aspects of a support assistant's work which contribute towards supporting a pupil with a medical need or a physical disability.

Physical management issues – these may include:

- on site access and mobility;
- personal hygiene routines;
- oversight in the playground;
- implementing exercise programme;
- monitoring of seating position;
- administering medication and monitoring of medical supplies;
- checking and storaging of specialist equipment;
- assisting with feeding;
- operating equipment, such as hoists and stairclimbers;
- liaising with outside agencies, e.g. occupational therapist, physiotherapist, and school nurse;
- developing independence skills.

Classroom/curriculum support issues:

- work on a 1:1 basis and in small groups;
- set up equipment;
- note key points;
- act as a scribe or amanuensis;
- give verbal prompting;
- organise worksheets and resources;
- support alternative recording strategies, e.g. tape recorder, photocopy notes;
- implement a speech and language therapy programme;
- developing independent working skills;
- carrying out physical tasks under the pupil's direction, e.g. D&T;
- preparing differentiated materials under the guidance of the subject teacher.

General considerations

- The support assistant should be engaged in promoting independence at all times. It will not be necessary for the support assistant to work alongside the pupil in all lessons.

- The support assistant should take notes during curriculum delivery in order to reinforce key points at a later stage in the lesson. Care must be taken to allow the pupil to focus on the teacher and not the support assistant. Consider the support assistant's seating position within the room.

- The support assistant should work under the direction of the SENCO and individual subject teachers.

- In practical sessions, when the pupil requires support to manipulate specialised equipment, the support assistant should work under the pupil's direction.

- Communication with outside agencies should be noted and passed on to the SENCO.

- Withdrawal of pupils for physical management routines should be negotiated with the SENCO and individual subject teachers.

- The support assistant may be asked to keep a written record to monitor the pupil in terms of stamina and physical performance. Home/school liaison should be established under the guidance of the SENCO/Head of Year.

- The support assistant may easily become isolated from the rest of the team if a high percentage of the support is given on a one to one basis. Be aware that support staff may require emotional support, especially if they work with pupils who have a deteriorating medical condition.

Alternative recording strategies

Pupils may experience writing difficulties for a number of reasons, reduced muscle strength, excessive fatigue and limited use of hand/upper limb resulting in poor letter formation and lack of fluency.

Initially, it would help to check the following areas, prior to remediation:

- sitting posture (see classroom management);
- pencil grip – is the pupil's grip unorthodox and tense? (see fine motor equipment);
- visual perception (check spatial awareness, body image);
- fine and gross motor co-ordination (check motor skill level, hand/eye co-ordination etc.).

The strategies to support recording listed below may be initiated alongside a programme to remediate handwriting, e.g. 'Write from the Start'. Alternatively, if the pupil has more significant physical difficulties, they should be started immediately on entry to school.

Primary level (KS1)

1. Teach the placement of letters on the computer keyboard using a drill and rote programme (improves hand/eye co-ordination, upper/lower case letter matching and recognition).

2. Use word banks to create sentences/magnetic letters and numbers to create words in literacy and sums in number work.

3. Give the pupil work in 'cloze' procedure format, i.e. the pupil rings the correct word, or have a number of individual words from which they can make a selection.

4. Use a cassette recorder for verbal evidence of attainment.

5. Act as the pupil's scribe, or arrange collaborative working sessions where another pupil does the writing.

6. Use Clicker 4 which is, in effect, an on-screen concept keyboard and requires only reasonable mouse skills to select words or letters. A wide range of grids is available to support many areas of the curriculum and new grids can be created very quickly and easily.

7. Provide the pupil with a numbers' printing set for number work.

8. Use simple computer programs requiring selection by either space bar or the number line (consult the mathematics adviser if necessary).

Primary level (KS2)

1. Continue with 2-8 above if appropriate.

2. If competence is developing on the keyboard, investigate the possible use of a word processor for lengthy writing tasks. If you anticipate that the pupil will be reliant on a word processor at secondary level, teach touch-typing skills in preparation.

3. Encourage the pupil to continue to write small amounts with the emphasis on *quality* rather than *quantity*.

4. Give multiple-choice questions.

Secondary level KS3 & 4

As above but also:

1. Allow greater use of word processing to support homework, as well as work in school.

2. For pupils who are more physically disabled investigate drawing/CAD packages to support D&T modules.

3. Photocopy a friend's notes if extensive note-taking is required.

4. Provide handouts prepared by the teacher, giving the main points.

5. Continue to encourage the use of a cassette recorder for homework.

6. Teach the pupil who has good spelling skills, but is simply slow at recording, to develop his/her own form of 'speed writing' using contracted words, e.g. $prod^d$ = produced, $prod^g$ = producing, $prod^n$ = production.

7. In Y10 voice recognition programs may also be considered if the pupil has good dictation and literacy skills that enable him/her to recognise mistakes and correct them.

8. Teach the pupil how to make more concise and effective notes or 'mind webs' to reduce the amount of writing required, e.g.

Not *this* –

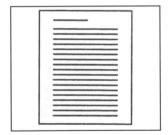

but this –

or this

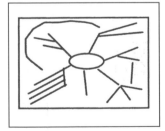

Specialised fine motor equipment

For those pupils who have difficulties in developing handwriting and manipulating standard classroom equipment, e.g. pencils, pens, scissors, rulers and compass, adapted equipment is available to promote skills and confidence.

To support the development of handwriting

The standardised tripod grip is not always the most comfortable for some pupils. However, the pencil grip must be relaxed and secure enough to allow them to produce a lengthy piece of writing.

A grip should be changed only if it is tense, looks uncomfortable and causes pain after writing for ten or more minutes.

Generally, pupils who wrap their thumbs or index fingers around the barrel of the pencil, have an *insecure* grasp and would benefit from remediation. One alternative is to hold the pencil between index and middle fingers (the Monk's grip).

Set aside some time to assess the pupil's pen/pencil grip.

- You will need a range of pencils with different-sized barrels (including maxi and triangular) for pupils to trial.

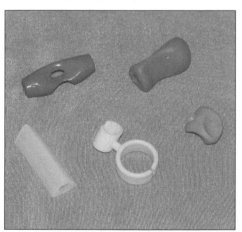

- A selection of pencil grips should also be available – most schools have triangular grips available for use but often a moulded grip, which requires pupils to position their fingers correctly, is more beneficial.

- From the bottom left clockwise in this picture, you can see the standard triangular grip, the Tri-go grip, the Ultra pencil grip, the 'Stubbi' or 'Stetro' grip and 'Grip it', (used by putting the ring on to the index finger).

- A range of pens is also needed to try out – including gel ink pens as well as ballpoints, some with rubberised grips, since they each have a different 'feel' and what suits one pupil may not suit another.

- Sometimes the provision of an angled-board improves writing – see 'Classroom organisation'.

- To stop paper or books from sliding on the desk use either Blu-Tack® or a rubberised non-slip mat.

Cutting skills

Low muscle tone or limited physical ability may result in poor scissor skills. There is a wide range of scissors now available for use. Classrooms should have a variety of scissors for pupils to select the most appropriate for their needs.

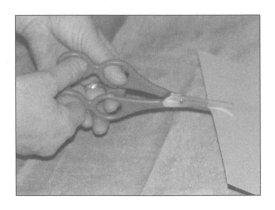

- The most difficult action is to open the scissors again once the pupil has completed the cut. 'Trainer' scissors allow him/her to use both hands for cutting (see right) giving extra leverage.

- Alternatively an adult may guide the pupil placing his/her fingers in the first set of handle holds over the top of the pupil's hand.

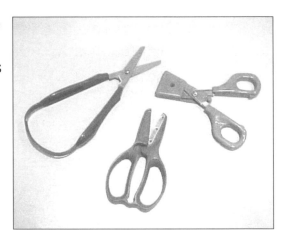

- These scissors are all self-opening. From the left clockwise the picture shows the Peta looped scissors, Peta spring-loaded scissors and Fiskars nursery scissors. The pupil uses the whole hand to close the blades giving maximum leverage.

- These increase confidence, especially if a pupil has low muscle tone and struggles to open and close standard scissors using two fingers only.

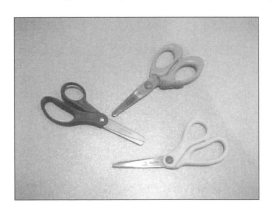

- With practice the pupil may progress to using scissors that have a larger lower handle, thereby improving leverage.

- The scissors shown here are Fiskars Junior scissors and Hetty and Milly from the Berol range.

- Pupils with more severe physical difficulties may require 'table top' scissors. These are self-opening scissors, either mounted on a wooden or plastic block or resting on the lower horizontal bar.

- The only action required is to push down on the top horizontal bar.

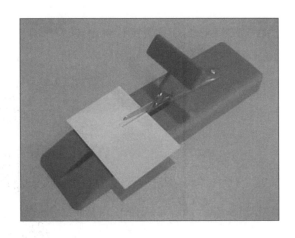

Supporting number work

- Some pupils have significant difficulties handling standard number equipment, e.g. Unifix™ cubes. These invariably end up on the floor, or the pupil loses count and does not develop a reliable counting pattern. This is simplified by using an abacus.

- When pupils begin to use a calculator they may repeatedly hit the wrong number. A large-buttoned calculator solves this difficulty.

- A large-buttoned scientific calculator can be found in the 'Accessories' menu within 'Windows' for those who need it.

- Additionally, there are a number of commercially-produced, 'on-screen calculator' programs for computers, that offer the facility of advanced calculations.

Other mathematics equipment

- Many pupils have difficulty using a standard ruler.

- Non-slip rulers can be found in a number of education catalogues. However, standard classroom rulers can be made non-slip by the simple addition of two small strips of 'self adhesive' Dycem™ (available from Nottingham Rehab or Homecraft) placed on the underside.

- A coloured sticker in the middle of the ruler also prompts the pupil to place his or her fingers in the correct position to draw a line. Holding the ruler at one end only, usually results in the other end being pulled down by the pressure of the pencil as it is drawn along it.

- For those pupils who have difficulty using a standard compass, the best alternative is the safe drawing compass, circle protractor or circle scribe. These can be used to draw circles of different diameters, the safe drawing compass also measures angles.

- A number of templates may be found in Art shops or catalogues to support lettering or design production for D&T or Art, e.g. for GCSE course work.

Science equipment

- Bug boxes that include integral magnifiers, make it easier for the pupil to handle specimens.

- Use fixed magnifiers, e.g. the QX3 Computer Microscope, which can be linked to the classroom PC. This allows the pupil much greater control over the images and magnification. They do not have to lean over the desk to look down the microscope.

- Additionally, effective use of clamps and test tube racks, gloves, aprons and goggles to cover safety issues, together with non-breakable (Pyrex) test tubes/beakers should be used.

Art

Try any of the following as appropriate:

- chunky crayons/pastels;
- thicker and shorter-handled paint brushes, including shaving brushes/decorating brushes;
- working at an easel or an adjustable-angled table, (see chapter on 'Adapted furniture') may be easier for pupils in wheelchairs;
- 'T-bar' brush holders;
- non-tip paint pots/holders;
- using clips/Dycem™ to keep work in place;
- printing with stamps rather than painting;
- Art/CAD programs to support design aspects;
- using 'clip art'/scanned images to support art modules.

Textiles

- provide large bodkins (metal or plastic) with bigger mesh materials;
- embroidery hoops remove the need for the pupil to hold the material;
- provide a needle threader.

Access to ICT

Pupils with limited physical ability, poor co-ordination, or low muscle tone may have problems using both the standard keyboard and mouse. Simply changing the settings in the 'Accessibility Options', 'Keyboard' or 'Mouse' menus etc. in the Controls panel may be sufficient to solve the problem.

Problems using keyboard	Solution
Pupil gets repeat letters/ deletions	Turn off or slow down the 'Auto-repeat' feature. *Settings – Control Panel – Keyboard – Speed*
The pupil can hit a key accurately but cannot hit the correct key.	Make a card 'mask' to fit over the keyboard. Reveal the target letter/s plus the space bar, delete and return. Continue to reveal letters one at a time until the pupil can type their full name, then remove the mask.
The pupil has difficulty activating two keys at the same time e.g. using the shift key to get a capital letter.	Turn on the 'StickyKeys' option, e.g. the pupil presses the shift key once and the next letter they select is a capital. *Settings – Control Panel – Accessibility Options – Keyboard*
The pupil has difficulty seeing the letters on the keys.	1. Raise the back of the keyboard, e.g. on a small angled board. 2. Purchase a set of yellow on black, or black on yellow stickers for the keys
Problems using the mouse	**Solution**
The pupil has difficulty seeing the cursor on screen.	1. Increase the size of the on-screen cursor. *Settings – Control Panel – Mouse – Pointers – select option* 2. Turn on 'Mouse tails' (the cursor leaves a visual trail). *Settings – Control Panel – Mouse – Motion – Pointer tails*
The cursor moves too quickly for them to control it.	1. Slow down the mouse speed. *Settings – Control Panel – Mouse – Motion – Pointer Speed* 2. It is also possible to use the number pad (all keys surrounding 5) on the keyboard to move the cursor – turn on Mouse keys. *Settings – Control Panel – Accessibility Options – Mouse*
The pupil finds it difficult to open programs using 'double click'.	1. Slow down the 'double click' speed. *Settings – Control Panel – Mouse – Double Click Speed* 2. Select the icon with a single click on the mouse and then press the 'Return' key.
The pupil finds it difficult to select menu/window options using the mouse.	Teach keyboard shortcuts, e.g. use the 'tab' key to scan through the menus, the up/down arrow keys to scroll through the options and return to select.
The pupil is left-handed or only has good use of the left hand.	Reverse the right and left button functions. *Settings – Control Panel – Mouse – Button Configuration*

Alternative keyboards and keyguards

For those pupils who miss-hit keys, e.g. hitting two keys at once or may hit the key above/below/beside, etc., the use of a keyguard should be investigated.

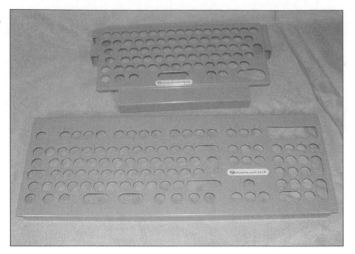

These are made of plastic or more frequently, metal and fit over the keyboard, usually attached by small pieces of velcro. The pupil can rest his/her hands on the keyguard and select the target letter through the correct hole.

There is a wide range of computer keyboards in use, all of which have slightly different dimensions, so a keyguard would have to be individually made to fit them. This can be costly and time consuming.

It is therefore easier and cheaper to purchase a keyboard and keyguard as a single unit.

Full-sized keyboards are available (top right).

However, there are reduced-sized keyboards, e.g. the 'Cherry' keyboard or the AlphaSmart (seen with optional keyguard). This may be used as a personal word processor, or for keyboard emulation linked to a PC if required.

For pupils whose *range* of movement is very limited, or who may require a more discreet word processor, smaller keyboards are available.

There is a whole range of Palmtops now available, e.g. the Psion range (lower left above), which may be selected depending on the intended use. These can be used for either independent word processing, or again to provide keyboard emulation.

Some pupils require a keyboard with much larger keys, e.g. the Jumbo Board available in upper or lower case (see right).

For those pupils who need a keyguard the Big Keys range has an ABC keyboard as well as the standard QWERTY layout. These are available with, or without keyguards. A keyboard glove can also be purchased if required.

Big Keys LX has punctuation keys, which are not on the entry level Big Keys keyboards.

Pupils may also be unable to use a standard mouse effectively despite practice. Trackerballs, which are available in all shops and catalogues, provide greater control. The pupil can operate the trackerball with one hand and press the selection button with the other.

Trackerballs may be simple and relatively cheap (see right).

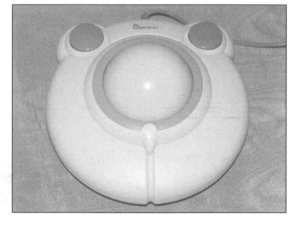

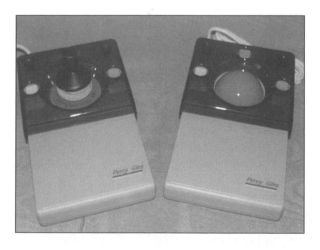

However, if the pupil has a greater physical difficulty, the Penny and Giles Rollerball or Joystick (see below) may be the best option.

These have a latching button at the top that requires a one press activation. A second press releases the 'drag' effect.

Both of these mouse emulation devices are now available with switch sockets to replace the left/right and drag button activation.

It may be necessary to request advice from the paediatric occupational therapist regarding the best positioning of equipment, especially for those pupils with a limited range of movement.

Accessing the PE curriculum

The National Curriculum acknowledges the entitlement of all pupils to a broad and balanced PE programme that will help to develop their motor competence and confidence, in both physical and social skills.

- The National Curriculum suggests that wherever possible, disabled pupils should be educated alongside their able-bodied peers without altering the activity.

- Where this is not possible, altering the rules, or modifying the equipment should make the activity accessible. An *alternative* activity should only be offered if *modification* is not possible.

- If an *alternative* activity is offered it should provide an educational experience and must not be a trivial or demeaning activity for the pupil.

The following information should be gathered and taken into consideration when planning activities:

1. Specific information about how the pupil is affected by his/her condition;

2. Activities that have been recommended by the doctor or physiotherapist;

3. Contra-indicated activities, those that must not be attempted for medical reasons;

4. Special considerations related to the condition, e.g. the pupil with an indwelling catheter, with a urine bag strapped to the leg, would be more appropriately dressed in jogging pants, rather than shorts;

5. Availability and deployment of additional adult support;

6. Level of independence skills such as dressing/undressing.

General considerations

- Consider the disabled pupil during the planning and introductory part of the lesson. Ask the pupil for his/her opinion. Ask the class for ideas about how the activity could be modified to include everybody.

- Consider the language used, e.g.
  - end and receive instead of *throw* and *catch*
  - *travel* instead of *run*
  - *travel with ball* instead of *dribbling*

- Consider including the disabled pupil in the skill element of the teaching session, but provide a modified 'small group' activity during team games.

Hockey

- Where possible, feet or wheelchair footplates can be used instead of hockey sticks.

- The use of Unihoc sticks on a hard surface enables most active pupils in wheelchairs to participate. If necessary, sticks could be attached to wheelchairs, so that the pupil has to manoeuvre the chair in order to hit the ball.
- Pupils in powered wheelchairs could play in goal with a reduced goal area.
- Mark out a tackle-free zone or a 'no go' area in front of the goal, to help unsteady pupils to play goalkeeper and be fully involved in the game, without worrying about being knocked over.
- Give pupils defined areas of play to ensure that slower pupils get an opportunity to play the ball and are able to do so, without the threat of being knocked.
- If pupils are playing in wheelchairs, it is important that sticks are not raised above knee height.

Netball

- Insist that all team members must touch the ball before attempting to shoot.
- Chalk a circle on the ground in the shooting area. To score a goal, bounce the ball in the chalked circle.
- Reduce the goal height.
- Provide a partner or 'buddy' for the disabled pupil who can catch the ball and feed it to his/her partner.

Football

- Allow pupils to use sticks or crutches to hit the ball.
- Create extra positions that will not involve too much running.
- A 'no go' area in front of the goal can help unsteady pupils to play goalkeeper and be fully involved in the game, without worrying about being knocked over.
- Give pupils defined areas of play to ensure that slower pupils get an opportunity to play the ball and are able to do so without the threat of being knocked.
- Provide an oversized ball which will not get trapped underneath footplates, if a wheelchair-user is playing.

Rounders/cricket

- Use a larger or softer ball. The ball can be hit with a larger bat, stick, feet or wheelchair.
- Provide alternative starting positions, e.g. balancing the ball on a cone, so that the disabled pupil can aim and hit, without having to cope with a bowler.
- Rounder runs can be scored by:
  - shortening the running area, e.g. arriving at second or third base;
  - having an extra post for the pupil to travel to;
  - making the fielders remain still for a count of 5, after the ball has been hit;
  - allowing powered-wheelchair users to use hockey sticks when fielding.

Athletics

- All throwing events can take place from standing/seating positions. Someone should hold wheelchairs to ensure that they do not tip over. When throwing, wheelchairs should be sideways on to the throwing area.

- Bean bags, wellingtons, tennis balls or clubs can be thrown instead of shots or discus.

- Javelins and bean bags can be directed to land on targets (precision events).

- Running and walking events, together with wheelchair dashes, 800m, 1500m races, are all suitable events.

- Wheelchair and electric wheelchair slalom courses are easy to set up, using skittles/cones.

- Pupils who participate in wheelchairs can be involved in measuring and recording the length of their 'jump', a jump being performed by a single push of a wheelchair between a marked set of tramlines.

- When hurdling, one is required to travel up and over an obstacle. The use of 'sleeping policemen' (preferably constructed of wood), will enable pupils participating in wheelchairs to go up and over an obstacle.

- Swimming may provide pupils who cannot experience travelling distances over land, an appropriate and meaningful alternative activity.

Racquet games including tennis and table tennis

- Co-operative rallying games may be more appropriate than competitive games.

- Reduce the playing area.

- Operate a scoring system, whereby points are scored if the ball arrives within reach of the disabled player.

- Provide alternative 'tees', such as a cone, as an alternative to serving in tennis.

- Provide alternative bats – larger or lighter; experiment with Velcro straps to prevent the bat or racquet being dropped.

- Provide alternative balls, which are lighter or slow moving.

- Play without a net.

- Use table barriers to play 'side table tennis'. Lengths of plywood attached to the table, or PE mats leaning up against the table, keep the ball in the 'play' area for longer, thereby reducing the frustration factor.

Substitute activities might include:

1. Snooker bowls

Bowls can be played on a snooker table. Each player uses two coloured balls. The game is started by the first player rolling the white ball to any spot on the table. The same player then rolls one of the coloured balls, trying to get it as near the white as possible, but it must rebound off at least two cushions. Alternative shots are then played and the player who finishes nearest the white, wins the 'end' and starts the next game.

2. Carpet bowls

These are played with two-and-a-half-inch diameter woods, obtainable from local sports shops.

3. Petanque

This is played with plastic or foam balls. The use of chutes (made from guttering), enables pupils with limited movement to participate.

4. Boccia

This is a simple form of bowls using light, pliable balls and a chute (see right).

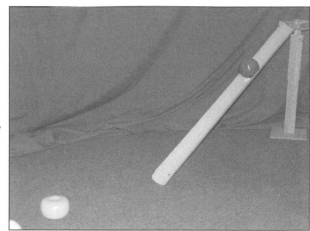

5. Darts

It is possible to place the dartboard at a low level or on the floor. Safety dartboards are available with soft tip darts.

6. Skittles

These are played with plastic skittles and plastic or foam balls. Balls can be rolled, kicked or hit using bats or sticks.

7. Polybat

This is similar to table tennis and can be played on a table tennis table. The set includes 8 side panels, table clips, an airflow ball and 2 polybats (see right).

8. Orienteering

School-based orienteering courses should follow a wheelchair-friendly route.

9. Fitness programme

Specific fitness programmes, designed to prove knowledge of good fitness habits for future life, should be devised. These should include advice from the physiotherapist, if appropriate.

10. Circuit training

Weight-training/circuit-training programmes could be arranged for older pupils.

10. Wheelchair-proficiency work

ROSPA provides a graded wheelchair proficiency training programme.

For further information contact:

www.youthsport.net – useful ideas, resources and information about sports including the rules for Boccia and table cricket.

www.britishwheelchairsport.org – contact specialist trainers for advice about specific sports. Useful contact for pupils who are wheelchair users.

www.teachernet.gov – a range of materials including lesson plans.

www.efds.co.uk – English Federation of Disability Sport – produces a magazine focusing solely on sport for disabled people.

www.snookergames.co.uk – Rules of bowls as played on a snooker table.

Ref: BT Top Sport, Youth Sport Trust "Including Young Disabled People" Handbook

Accessing Design and Technology

Points to consider when differentiating the Design and Technology curriculum to include pupils with physical difficulties:

1. set finely graded specific objectives, e.g.
   - to be able to select equipment for measuring and marking wood;
   - to be able to give accurate instructions to CSA to facilitate cutting wood;

2. consider deployment of support staff for each activity, e.g.
   - support staff to work with an individual pupil or a small group of pupils;
   - support staff to modify/enlarge/simplify class work sheets;

3. agree recording strategies with support staff, which will inform your assessment of pupils' work;
   - brief written notes by the support assistant can enable teachers to have an accurate record of support given in each lesson;

4. ensure all practical work is pupil led:
   - when support staff are assisting with practical tasks the support assistant must work under the direction of the pupil;

5. assess work using the same criteria as for other pupils:
   - if a pupil has given correct instructions to their support assistant then credit them for their knowledge and understanding;

6. consider classroom organisation and equipment storage:
   - a wheelchair user will require a workbench of an appropriate height;
   - an individual tool set will minimise movement within the classroom;
   - make other pupils aware of safety implications of a pupil working in a wheelchair; the wheelchair user is vulnerable at this height;

7. consider special arrangements for examinations:
   - pupils with additional physical needs are entitled to have the same assistance in examinations as they have in lessons;
   - these arrangements can include a practical assistant, additional time, use of an amanuensis, rest periods and separate facilities;
   - further details are available from individual examination boards on the QCA website and 'GCSE Examinations: Implications for candidates with cerebral palsy and associated disabilities', Scope Advisory Assessment Service (updated annually).

8. consider working out of key stage:
   - pupils may work from the programmes of study of a lower key stage to enable them to progress and demonstrate achievement;
   - work should be presented in a context suitable to a pupil's age.

No cost/low cost adaptations – food

- Ensure at least one set of equipment is stored at an accessible height.

- Provide a perching stool if the pupil is standing for prolonged periods or if balance is a problem.

- Request advice from the occupational therapy service regarding use of standard equipment.

- Seek advice from the relevant educational support service regarding specialist equipment.

Pupils who have good use of one hand can use the auto chopper instead of a knife to chop vegetables.

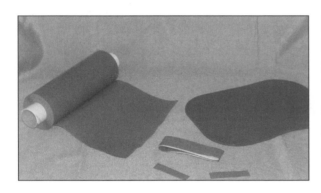

Damp tea towels can help to stabilise a mixing bowl. Dycem™ non-slip mats are useful for anchoring a range of equipment. They are available in two thicknesses. Thick mats are useful for trays, chopping boards and heavy mixing bowls. The thin variety is supplied on a roll and can be cut to size.

The knob turner can be used for turning taps or knobs on a cooker. It comprises a series of retractable metal pins that mould to the shape of the object, providing a firm grip. This would be useful for pupils who have limited hand strength or reduced grip resulting from arthritis.

The sandwich spreader board hooks over the edge of the table and enables pupils to spread butter using one hand.

Vegetable holding boards are available which incorporate a grater and spikes to hold a vegetable whilst peeling it.

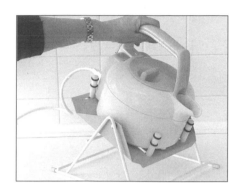

The kettle tilt can be used to ensure safe pouring of hot liquids. They are available in a variety of shapes and can be used to hold jugs and teapots.
A useful safety tip: encourage pupils who have tremors to stand their receptacle on a tray; if there are any spills they won't go on the floor.

A panhandle holder allows pupils to stir without holding the panhandle.

Medium cost adaptations – food or resistant materials

- Use electrical equipment that duplicates a manual function, e.g. food processor for chopping vegetables, rubbing-in method for pastry, creaming sugar and fat for cakes.

- Use a mounting system for hand-held electrical tools. These may need to be designed and made by D&T technician.

- Use commercially-available clamps to stabilise work when marking and cutting.

- Provide an individual set of tools, possibly lightweight or junior versions, to be used by pupils with low muscle tone or weakness in their hands.

- Investigation is recommended for specialist equipment through specialist catalogues such as Nottingham Rehab or Smith and Nephew Homecraft.

Higher cost adaptations

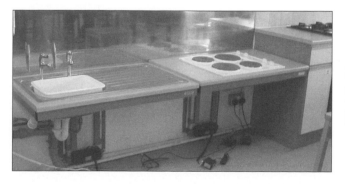

Use height-adjustable furniture and height-adjustable workstations including hob and sink to provide access for all pupils.

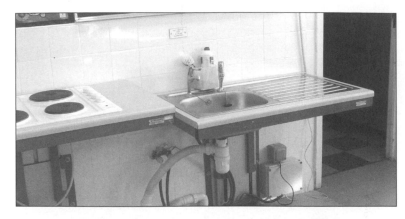

Pupils with short stature, those in wheelchairs and those in standing frames could benefit from access to a height adjustable sink.

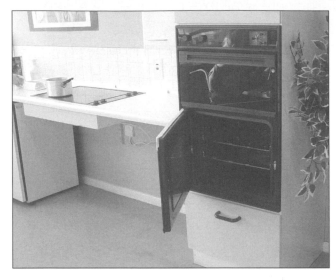

Wall-mounted, built-in oven with pull-out tray will protect the wheelchair user's legs.

A combination microwave oven on an accessible work surface would negate the need for an oven.

Leave an open kick board space to allow for wheelchair footplates.

Pull-out storage racks in cupboards are easy to access.

Section 4

Developing skills for learning

Developing visual perception

Pupils with perceptual difficulties tend to bump into objects or people, have a poor understanding of the 3D world and its relationship to 2D pictures, and have problems acquiring the skills of reading and writing.

Classroom support for pupils with problems with visual perception

Staff should be aware that pupils demonstrating problems with visual perception may:

- have difficulty copying from the blackboard;
- be slow at reading and, therefore, reluctant to read aloud;
- find small text difficult to read;
- miss out words/lines when reading;
- have difficulties reading text in different fonts.

There are a variety of ways to support pupils in the classroom:

- Provide a quiet area, which is clear of decoration/stimulus, for the pupil to work in.
- Reduce visual clutter in displays.
- Provide simple, clear work sheets and activity cards.
- Enlarge text and use double spacing. If possible use the Sassoon Primary Infant Font (created for visual clarity for primary-aged pupils).
- For some pupils print work sheets on a coloured background to reduce the 'glare' of white paper.
- If the pupil has to do a drawing, give him/her a frame to work within (helps contain work and aids positioning on the page).
- Seating position in class is important. The pupil should sit facing the blackboard and teacher, (not at an angle to it, since this distorts visual perception), for all copying work.
- Using a fixed-angled board also helps since there is reduced eye movement between model and reproduction.
- When writing allow the pupil to write on alternate lines since this reduces visual clutter.
- Holding a book upright when reading reduces visual distortion of text.
- Point to each word or use a piece of card, or a ruler, to highlight the line being read.
- The pupil may need to work through 'Write from the Start', a perceptuo-motor programme that helps all the areas of skill development required to aid writing.

Problems with:	Try the following:
Spatial organisation difficulties (i.e. visuo-spatial awareness) **Check:** Does the pupil have a good understanding of positional words, up, down, in front of, behind, above, below, between, beside? Can he/she move forwards, backwards, sideways, clockwise, anti-clockwise, to the right/left, on request?	Begin with gross motor activities (movement through space); • make obstacle courses (increase difficulty), slalom courses, mazes (ask the pupil to verbalise moves), team games. Then hand/eye co-ordination tasks (reduced movement in limited space); • threading/lacing/pegboard patterns/ building with Lego; • when beginning writing, put a finger or space template between words.
Form constancy The understanding that an object stays the same regardless of position in space, e.g. reducing in size in the distance.	• matching pairs; • shape recognition/classification by shape, colour, size, etc; • ring the odd one out, same/different; • use small cut-out shapes to create bigger shapes/pictures (using a template to begin with, then without); • copy a shape/complete the drawing of shape or object.
Orientation and laterality Reversals seen (left/right, top/bottom). **Check:** Eye dominance – if the pupil has cross laterality i.e. right-handed and left eye dominant, he/she may experience the following problems: • developing left/right orientation on the page; • reversals of letters or words; • mixing left and right sides of the body; • be slow to develop hand dominance.	Use a multi-sensory approach: • involve touch and sight using three dimensional letters, or LDA 'Roll and Write' letters; • give visual perception exercises, e.g. ring all the letter 'b's; • have one pupil write a letter on the back of another pupil, who should identify the letter – get him/her to talk through the movements as he/she is forming them; – **N.B.** 'up' and 'down' have more relevance in this situation because of the vertical position for the activity; • use 'word play' prompts, e.g. bat and ball (for 'b').
Figure/ground discrimination (problems with focus resulting from too much visual stimulus).	• mosaics, inset boards, jigsaws, etc.; • pick out/colour/objects in busy pictures; • play spot the difference; • recognise an object/picture as it is gradually revealed.

Memory skills

To develop short- and long-term memory skills:

- Provide a list of topic/subject-related words at the onset of each term – this helps parents to know what is going to be covered, it helps pupils who take time assimilating new vocabulary and provides material for spelling development.

- Provide coloured pens/ encourage use of coloured pens – colour helps stimulate visual memory, improves clarity of notes, highlights key words and word associations. These are fun to use and this encourages reluctant writers.

- Create summary cards of topic material when each topic is completed, to aid over-learning and revision.

- Provide wall displays of key terminology to help those with weak spelling and/or weak word association skills.

- Encourage pupils or support staff to write key words on individual Post-it® stickers. These can then be arranged in an appropriate order and discarded when used.

- Maintain the use of a planner/diary to help the pupil remember specific items.

- Consider sound levels in classroom. Background hubbub can be extremely distracting for some pupils. Background music can help screen out background noise and can aid concentration.

- Ensure pupils know the purpose of tasks, particularly homework. This can help them focus on appropriate factors.

- Beware of overloading the working memory. Pupils with reading, listening, spelling and writing difficulties are easily overloaded, leading to confusion, frustration and reduced transference to long-term memory.

- Encourage use of 'mind-maps' for each module of work, to give an overview of work covered and to aid revision or over-learning.

Attention and listening skills

Some pupils may have poor attention and listening skills related to their medical condition. The following suggestions should be considered:

- Say the pupil's name first and gain his/her attention before giving instructions or information.

- Ensure instructions are at the pupil's level of understanding, e.g. two/three word level of understanding.

- Ensure work is at the appropriate, differentiated to the pupil's level.

- Assess how many instructions the pupil can follow and use cue cards to give a pictorial prompt for the sequence of actions required in an activity.

- Give time for the pupil to process the information.

- Reduce visual stimulation around the pupil's workspace and ensure that it is away from the window, displays, etc.

- Remove distractions, e.g. objects on the desk which can be fiddled with instead of listening. Alternatively provide a material which can be manipulated without causing a distraction, e.g. Blu-Tack™.

- Seat the pupil near to the teacher in order to promote good listening and attention skills. Use a visual signal to give reminders.

- Set tasks which match the pupil's ability to concentrate on a task. Work on extending his/her concentration span in the pupil's IEP.

- Younger pupils can be involved in activities to develop listening skills:
  - simple lotto games matching everyday objects which make sounds to pictures, e.g. the adult squeaks a plastic duck behind their back and the child matches it to the appropriate picture;
  - following actions in rhymes;
  - playing games such as 'Simon says...'.

Developing organisational skills

Some pupils will need support to develop organisational skills. Others may need strategies to overcome difficulties. The following are suggestions that may help:

- Provide a method of showing the structure of the day through a visual timetable, diary.

- Give pictorial task cards to aid organisational skills, e.g. a card to show in which order clothes should be put on, dressing after PE, prompt cards to indicate equipment needed for a lesson, or have a mat with templates of the equipment which is needed for an activity.

- Some pupils may need extra support to organise themselves in class, e.g. at tidy-up time, after group input, by receiving extra instructions in a simple manner.

- Help the pupil to develop organisational skills by providing cue cards for different activities, individually or on a flip chart for a group of pupils:

For this activity you will need your:

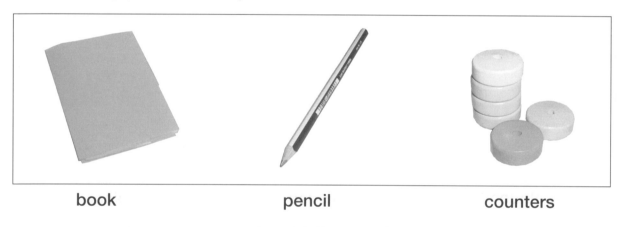

| book | pencil | counters |

- Encourage parents to make their child's belongings more easily distinguished by the use of a particular logo or colour, clearly labelled with his/her name.

- Encourage parents to buy school bags with different compartments to enable each one to be used for a different organisational function, e.g. PE equipment, dinner money, subject wallets.

- Differentiate subjects by colour, match to colour spots on the timetable, back text books in a colour to match the subject.

- Use clear plastic wallets to pack equipment for each subject, colour-matched, which may result in duplication of equipment but make for simpler organisation at the beginning and end of each lesson, e.g. pen, compass, ruler, calculator in a maths wallet.

- Ensure the pupil has noted homework requirements in some form, e.g. teacher noting work, use of a Dictaphone™.

- Use a home/school diary to encourage equipment and homework to be brought to school at the correct time.

- Suggest to parents that they encourage their child to develop organisational skills at home by having a white board near the door, with reminders of what is needed when packing their bags the night before.

- Pupils may need support for organisation at lunch time, e.g. collecting a lunch tray whilst carrying a bag and then finding a seat.

- Use a plan of the school to help movement around the site.

Supporting emotional issues

There are a large variety of emotional issues related to medical conditions and these are also interlinked with issues of self-esteem and establishing positive peer group relationships.

Issues which may arise	Strategies and practical help
frustration at restrictions brought about by the condition, e.g. not being able to participate in sports	• allow discussion of frustrations with school staff and ensure that the pupil has access to as many activities as possible within the limitations of his/her condition; • look for alternative activities.
instances of bullying or teasing	• ensure that the pupil's concerns related to bullying and teasing, are addressed; • use circle time as a forum for raising and addressing the issues of bullying and teasing; • consider the use of 'circle of friends'.
depression, resentment, anger; anxiety about the condition; appearance of new symptoms; recurrence of symptoms; feelings of being 'different'.	• ensure the pupil has access to a professional, e.g. a member of staff or specialist nurse, who can discuss the issues related to the condition; • ensure regular feedback to parents.
the need for permanent medication and treatments can be a dominant factor	• enable the pupil to regard treatments and medication as an accepted part of his/her life, by dealing with it in a 'matter of fact' way; • provide easy access to treatment or medication, water, snacks and all other factors in the health care plan; • encourage the pupil to be open with his/her peers; • allow friends to accompany them where appropriate.

interruption of schooling through hospitalisation and treatments	• ensure the pupil is made welcome on his/her return; • encourage peers, e.g. the 'buddy' system, to help his/her back into normal routines; • consider how work that has been missed will be made up – teacher/student notes being passed on, extra tuition.
embarrassment at some of the more obvious symptoms	• use occasions such as PHSE or circle time (if the pupil/or parents are happy with this).
dealing with fluctuating condition – 'good days', 'bad days'	• encourage all concerned to have empathy, e.g. peers, other adults, and plan accordingly; • watch for indicators and reduce demands on the pupil accordingly; • encourage the pupil/parents to take professional advice; • encourage older pupils to be self-limiting.
feelings connected with deterioration in condition, e.g. grief, fear.	• be prepared to engage in pupil-led discussion, being sensitive to the level of understanding, depth of questioning and parental wishes; • recognise that it may not be possible to answer all the questions; • provide a place in school where the pupil can have some 'space'.
death of a peer with a similar condition	• all adults concerned with pupils facing deteriorating conditions, should have access to support, further information and training, e.g. Lost for Words training (see over); • when another pupil with the same condition dies, anticipate that the pupil will exhibit emotions and may wish to talk, cry or be given space to deal with this in his/her own way; • allow friends to find a way of supporting each other.
being over-burdened by other people's emotions, i.e. parents, peers, teachers, etc.	• try to provide as normal a routine as possible; • give an explanation to the class, when the pupil is not present.

Be aware that many of the issues may be relevant to other pupils in the class who may need reassurance, explanations and support.

School staff will require training for issues related to pupils with medical conditions, in order to support pupils in their care.

Staff will not always feel that they have answers but should be as sensitive as possible.

Further information

Lost for Words
A training package for teachers
Learning Services
Kingston upon Hull

Tel: 01482 613423

Coping with Bereavement:
A handbook for teachers,
John Holland,
Cardiff Academic Press
St Fagans Road
Fairwater
Cardiff CF5 3AE

Tel: 01222 554909

Finding a Way Through When
Someone Close has Died:
A workbook by young people for
young people,
Pat Mood and Lesley Whittaker.

Interventions with Bereaved Children,
Susan C. Smith and Margaret Pennells.

Helping Children to Manage Loss:
Positive strategies for renewal and growth,
Brenda Mallon.

The above are available from:
Jessica Kingsley Publishers
116 Pentonville Road, London N1 9JB

Tel: 020 7833 2307

Developing a positive self-image

A pupil who has a positive self-image will have the confidence to deal with difficulties related to their condition and be more confident in new situations. Schools should adopt measures, some of which are listed below, to promote such an image.

- Have a positive attitude to the pupil.

- Ensure that all staff are made aware of the pupil's condition, the implications and the considerations needed to meet the pupil's needs.

- Meet the needs in an unobtrusive manner.

- Be sensitive to the pupil's needs and aware of their limitations, whilst not letting it be an excuse for inappropriate behaviour.

- It may be appropriate to inform other peers of the pupil's medical condition (in accordance with the pupils' and parents' wishes) in order for them to have understanding.

- Close friends may play a role in supporting the pupil in some way, e.g. carrying a tray, accompanying between classes, passing on notes for lessons missed due to absence related to the medical condition.

- Bullying and teasing should not be tolerated.

- Have an assigned member of staff as a 'listening ear', for those pupils who find this useful.

- Work should be at an appropriate level to the pupil, possibly addressed in an IEP, but not necessarily, as some pupils will not have learning difficulties related to their condition. Achievement will increase confidence.

- If self-esteem needs a boost it may be useful to give some responsibility to the pupil, e.g. monitor, 'buddy'.

- Use displays as a way of celebrating achievement across the ability range.

- Ensure that pupils are not penalised for absences related to their medical condition, e.g. when class points are gained for attendance.

- Teacher assessment should be used for internal testing, if frequent absence affects attainment grades.

125

Glossary

Ataxia	failure of muscle co-ordination resulting in irregular and jerky movement
Atrophy	wasting of any part of the body
Autonomic shock syndrome	an emergency condition requiring immediate attention. Occurs in people with spinal cord injuries at or above T-6 (thoracic/neck). An abnormal response to a problem usually bowel or bladder. Can be as a result of pressure sores, broken skin, burns, and ingrown toenails
Contracture	limitation in the range of movement
Diplegia	paralysis in corresponding limbs
Encopresis	stool incontinence
Enuresis	bladder incontinence
External fixator	metal frame to hold bones in place
Hemiplegia	paralysis or weakness of one side of the body
Hyperglycemia	high blood sugar
Hypertonic	increased muscle tone
Hypoglycemia	low blood sugar
Hyponic	decreased muscle tone
Lateral confusion	reversals in letters and numbers; mixing of letter order within words (as opposed to spelling errors); bizarre writing, drawing and spelling
Motor planning	the ability to plan and execute motor movements
Occlusion	blockage
Paraplegia	paralysis of the lower half of the body
Quadriplegia	paralysis of all four limbs
Spastic	increased muscle tone
Talipes	club foot
Tremor	regular repetitive movements
Visuo-motor skills	the ability to reproduce that which is seen, e.g. copying shapes, matching, tracing and sorting
Visuo-spatial ability	the ability to judge distances, to appreciate terms such as 'nearer than' 'farther than', 'wider', 'narrower', 'lower', 'higher', to understand directionality, left right discrimination, orientation

IHCP for a pupil with medical needs

Name: ....

....

Date of Birth:...

Condition: ....

....

....

....

....

....

Photograph

Class/Form:... Date: ....

Name of School:... Review date: ....

Contact Information:

Family Contact 1	**Family Contact 2**
Name	Name ....
Phone no. (work)	Phone no. (work) ....
(home)	(home) ....
Relationship	Relationship ....

Clinic/Hospital Contact	**G.P.**
Name	Name ....
Phone no.	Phone no. ....

Describe condition and give details of pupil's individual symptoms: ....

....

....

....

Name: .... Date of birth: ....

Daily care requirements:

....

....

....

....

....

Describe what constitutes an emergency for the pupil and the action to be taken if this occurs:

....

....

....

Follow up care: ....

....

....

Who is responsible in an emergency (state if different on off site activities): ....

....

....

Form circulated to:

☐ Admin team/pupil file

☐ Class teacher and support staff

☐ Pupil information file for supply teachers

☐ School nurse

☐ Parents

Date: .... Review: ....

Some professionals who may be involved

Professional	Personnel and contact number
Educational Psychologist	
Special Educational Needs Support Service	
Educational Service for Physical Disability	
Speech and Language Therapist	
Education Service for the Visually Impaired	
Education Service for the Hearing Impaired	
Senior Clinical Medical Officer (SCMO)	
School Nurse	
Physiotherapist	
Occupational Therapist	
Paediatric Specialist Nurse	
Support Groups	

Suppliers

List of suppliers	Tel. Number/Web/Email	Equipment
Advanced Stairlift (Scotland) Ltd Unit 3, Burnside Business Court North Road Inverkeithing Fife, Scotland KY11 1NZ	01383 411400 www.advancedstairlifts.co.uk	Stair Climber demonstrations
Atkinson Vari-tech Ltd Unit 4 Sett End Road Shadsworth Blackburn Lancashire BB1 2PT	01254 678777 www.vari-tech.co.uk	Variable height tables to support Art, D&T, ICT
Bishop Sports and Leisure Bishop House East Burnham Park Crown Lane Farnham Royal Slough, Berkshire SL2 3SF	01753 648666 www.bishopsport.co.uk	PE equipment
Economatics (Education) Ltd Epic House Darnall Road Sheffield S9 5AA	0114 281 3311 www.economatics.co.uk	QX3 Computer Microscope
Galt Education & Pre-school Johnsonbrook Road Hyde, Cheshire SK1 4QT	08702 42 44 77 enquiries@galt-educational.co.uk	Adapted furniture, fine motor equipment
Hope Education Ltd Orb Hill Huddersfield Road Oldham, Lancs OL4 2ST	08702 433 400 www.hope-education.co.uk	Fine motor & PE equipment, adapted furniture

Inclusive Technology Ltd Gateshead Business Park Delph, Oldham OL3 5BX	01457 819790 www.inclusive.co.uk	Equipment to support ICT
Innovations in Sport Davies Sport Excelsior Road Ashby Park Ashby de la Zouch Leicestershire LE65 1NG	0845 1204 515 www.daviessports.co.uk	PE equipment
LDA Duke Street Wisbech Cambridgeshire PE13 2AE	01945 463441 www.instructionalfair.co.uk	Fine motor equipment
Maudesport Beecham Close Aldridge Walsall West Midlands WS9 8UZ	0870 3814000 www.maudesport.com	PE equipment
Nes Arnold Ludlow Hill Road West Bridgford Nottingham NG2 6HD	0845 1204 525 orders@nesarnold.co.uk	Fine motor & PE equipment, adapted furniture
Newitts Claxton Hall Flaxton York YO60 7RE	01904 468551 www.newitts.com	PE equipment
Nottingham Rehab Supplies Novara House Excelsior Road Ashby Park Ashby de la Zouch Leicestershire LE65 1NG	0845 1204 522 www.nrs-uk.co.uk	Adapted furniture, fine motor/PE/Food Technology equipment

Pressings & Presstool Engineering Unit 4, Tokenspire Park, Moorgate Road, Liverpool L33 7RX	0151 546 8786 www.pressings-presstool.co.uk	Food technology
ROMPA Ltd Goyt Side Road Chesterfield Derbyshire S40 2PH	0800 056 2323 www.rompa.com	Fine motor & PE equipment
SEMERC Granada Learning Ltd Granada Television Quay Street Manchester M60 9EA	0161 827 2927 www.semerc.com	Equipment to support ICT including computer trolleys
Smith & Nephew Homecraft Ltd PO Box 5665 Kirby-in-Ashfield Notts NG17 7QX	01623 721000 homecraft.sales@smith-nephew.com	Adapted furniture, fine motor, Food Tech equipment
Step by Step Lee Fold Hyde Cheshire SK14 4LL	0845 300 1089 sbs@stpbystp.demon.co.uk	Adapted furniture

Improve your support for pupils with SEN with other books in this series...

The books in this series gather together all the vital knowledge and practical support that schools need to meet specific special needs. Information is simply explained and clearly sign-posted so that practitioners can quickly access what they need to know. Each book describes a specific area of special educational need and explains how it might present difficulties for pupils within the school setting. Checklists and photocopiable forms are provided to help save time and develop good practice.

Supporting Children with Behaviour Difficulties
£10.00 • Paperback • 64 A4 pages • 1-84312-228-6 • July 2004

Supporting Children with Motor Co-ordination Difficulties
£10.00 • Paperback • 64 A4 pages • 1-84312-227-8 • July 2004

Supporting Children with Fragile X Syndrome
£10.00 • Paperback • 64 A4 pages • 1-84312-226-X • July 2004

Supporting Children with Speech and Language Difficulties
£10.00 • Paperback • 144 A4 pages • 1-84312-225-1 • July 2004

Supporting Children with Medical Conditions
£20.00 • Paperback • 144 A4 pages • 1-84312-224-3 • May 2004

Supporting Children with Epilepsy
£10.00 • Paperback • 64 A4 pages • 1-84312-223-5 • May 2004

Supporting Children with Dyslexia
£10.00 • Paperback • 48 A4 pages • 1-84312-222-7 • July 2004

Supporting Children with Down's Syndrome
£10.00 • Paperback • 48 A4 pages • 1-84312-221-9 • May 2004

Supporting Children with Cerebral Palsy
£10.00 • Paperback • 48 A4 pages • 1-84312-220-0 • May 2004

Supporting Children with Autistic Spectrum Disorder
£10.00 • Paperback • 64 A4 pages • 1-84312-219-7 • May 2004

Supporting Children with Asthma
£10.00 • Paperback • 48 A4 pages • 1-84312-218-9 • May 2004

ORDER FORM

Qty	ISBN	Title	Price	Subtotal
	1-84312-218-9	Supporting Children with Asthma	£10.00	
	1-84312-219-7	Supporting Children with ASD	£10.00	
	1-84312-228-6	Supporting Children with Behaviour Ds	£10.00	
	1-84312-220-0	Supporting Children with Cerebral Palsy	£10.00	
	1-84312-221-9	Supporting Children with Down's Syndrome	£10.00	
	1-84312-222-7	Supporting Children with Dyslexia	£10.00	
	1-84312-223-5	Supporting Children with Epilepsy	£10.00	
	1-84312-226-X	Supporting Children with Fragile X Syndrome	£10.00	
	1-84312-224-3	Supporting Children with Medical Conditions	£20.00	
	1-84312-227-8	Supporting Children with MCDs	£10.00	
	1-84312-225-1	Supporting Children with S&L Difficulties	£10.00	
	1-84312-204-9	David Fulton Catalogue	FREE	

Postage and Packing: FREE to schools, LEAs and other institutions.
£2.50 per order for private/personal orders.
Prices and publication dates are subject to change.

P&P		
TOTAL		

Please complete delivery details:

Name: ....

Organisation: ....

....

Address: ....

....

....

....

Postcode:..

Tel: ....

Email: ....

☐ Please add me to your email mailing list

Payment:

☐ Please invoice *(applicable to schools, LEAs and other institutions)*

☐ I enclose a cheque payable to David Fulton Publishers Ltd
(include postage and packing if applicable)

☐ Please charge to my credit card *(Visa/Barclaycard, Access/Mastercard, American Express, Switch, Delta)*

card number

expiry date

(Switch customers only) valid from   issue number

Send your order to our distributors:

**HarperCollins Publishers
Customer Service Centre
Westerhill Road • Bishopbriggs
Glasgow • G64 2QT**

Tel. 0870 787 1721

Fax. 0870 787 1723

or order online at
www.fultonpublishers.co.uk